PRAC
GOU

Com
Coming®

Chicken Favourites

Paré • Billey • Pirk • Darcy

Distributed by
Canada Book Distributors
www.canadabookdistributors.com
www.companyscoming.com
Tel: 1-800-661-9017

Library and Archives Canada Cataloguing in Publication

Title: Chicken favourites / Paré, Billey, Pirk, Darcy.
Other titles: Company's coming
Names: Paré, Jean, 1927– author. | Billey, Ashley, author. | Pirk, Wendy, 1973– author. | Darcy, James, 1956– author.
Identifiers: Canadiana 20210322926 | ISBN 9781988133928 (softcover)
Subjects: LCSH: Cooking (Chicken) | LCGFT: Cookbooks.
Classification: LCC TX750.5.C45 P3585 2022 | DDC 641.6/65—dc23

All cover photos by Company's Coming except: from GettyImages: Cover: ALLEKO; Front Flap, top: bhofack2.

All inside photos by Company's Coming except: from GettyImages: ALLEKO, 5; bhofack2, 47, 139; bonchan, 27; boophotography, 75; carlosrojas20, 97; DronG, 9; Elena_Danileiko, 125; evil_beau, 123; gbh007, 6; igorr1, 81; ivandzyuba, 127; Jarvna, 15; johncopland, 83; larik_malasha, 11; Lilechka75, 151; Mariha-kitchen, 19; Maria_Lapina, 31; Mizina, 93; MSPhotographic, 109; Ravsky, 107; Kseniya Romazanova, 113; Sapunovaphoto, 49; travellinglight, 99; Tatiana Volgutova, 155; Tetiana_Chudovska, 71; wmaster890, 111; Andrey Zhuravlev, 103.

We acknowledge the financial support of the Government of Canada.
Nous reconnaissons l'appui financier du gouvernement du Canada.

Funded by the Government of Canada
Financé par le gouvernement du Canada | Canada

PC: 38-1

Table of Contents

The Jean Paré Story

Jean Paré (pronounced "jeen PAIR-ee") grew up understanding that the combination of family, friends and home cooking is the best recipe for a good life. When Jean left home, she took with her a love of cooking, many family recipes and an intriguing desire to read cookbooks as if they were novels!

"Never share a recipe you wouldn't use yourself."

When her four children had all reached school age, Jean volunteered to cater the 50th anniversary celebration of the Vermilion School of Agriculture, now Lakeland College, in Alberta, Canada. Working from her home, Jean prepared a dinner for more than 1,000 people and from there launched a flourishing catering operation that continued for more than 18 years.

As requests for her recipes increased, Jean was often asked, "Why don't you write a cookbook?" The release of *150 Delicious Squares* on April 14, 1981, marked the debut of what would soon turn into one of the world's most popular cookbook series.

Company's Coming cookbooks are distributed in Canada, the United States, Australia and other world markets. Bestsellers many times over in English, Company's Coming cookbooks have also been published in French and Spanish.

Familiar and trusted in home kitchens around the world, Company's Coming cookbooks are offered in a variety of formats. Highly regarded as kitchen workbooks, the softcover Original Series, with its lay-flat plastic comb binding, is still a favourite among home cooks.

Jean Paré's approach to cooking has always called for quick and easy recipes using everyday ingredients. That view served her well, and the tradition continues in the Practical Gourmet series.

Jean's Golden Rule of Cooking is: Never share a recipe you wouldn't use yourself. It's an approach that has worked—millions of times over!

Introduction

Once considered second fiddle to beef as North America's favourite meat, chicken has now surpassed its bovine counterpart in popularity. It's easy to see why chicken is so popular. Not only is it delicious, but it is also a nutritious protein choice and extremely versatile. You can dress it up for company or dress it down for quick family meals. You can choose between dark or white meat, and cook it whole, ground or in separate pieces. It's equally delicious served hot or cold.

From a nutrition perspective, chicken is a terrific addition to a balanced diet. It is high in B vitamins and niacin and is a high quality protein. White meat is an excellent low-fat choice, depending on how it is prepared and especially once the skin is removed, and dark meat is high in iron and zinc.

For people who are concerned about the health of the environment, chicken is a natural choice because it has a smaller ecological footprint than beef or pork production.

To reflect chicken's popularity, we've put together this cookbook of favourite chicken dishes, including recipes for appetizers, soups, salads and entrees. We've also included tips on shopping, storing, cooking and carving your poultry, as well as safety guidelines for handling the meat.

Types of chicken

The different labels on whole chickens relate to their size:

- A **broiler** or **fryer** is a young chicken weighing 1.5 to 3.86 pounds (700 g to 1.75 kg).
- A **roaster** weighs more than 3.86 pounds (1.75 kg).
- A **stewing hen** is an older hen of about 5.5 pounds (2.5 kg), best suited for moist cooking methods such as braising and stewing.

Air-chilled vs. water-chilled

Both methods refer to the way poultry is cooled.

- **Air-chilling:** Chicken and turkey are placed on conveyor belts and cooling fans quickly reduce their temperature to less than 39.2°F (4°C).
- **Water- or immersion-chilling**: The meat is submerged in cold water to reduce the temperature quickly. Generally, if you don't see the label "air-chilled," it means that the poultry product has been water-chilled.

Substitution strategies

If a recipe calls for chicken breasts and your freezer's full of thighs, you can substitute, but keep the following in mind:

- If the recipe calls for a bone-in part, use a bone-in equivalent of the same weight.
- If the recipe calls for a boneless part, use a boneless equivalent of the same weight.
- Remember that white meat cooks more quickly than dark meat. Adjust cooking times accordingly.

TIPS

Smart shopping

- Choose cold, tightly-wrapped packages with no holes or tears.
- Pick up your poultry items just before you head to the checkout and get them home within 2 hours (1 hour if it's hot outside).
- Tuck packages of poultry into produce bags so they don't leak onto other groceries.

Fridge and freezer fundamentals

- Refrigerate or freeze poultry immediately. Store whole poultry and poultry parts in the fridge for up to 2 days and ground chicken for no more than 24 hours. Place the poultry on a plate or tray on the bottom shelf to prevent juices from contaminating other foods.
- To freeze, wrap fresh poultry packages with airtight heavy-duty foil, freezer wrap or freezer paper, or place the contents in freezer bags. If using freezer bags, press out as much air as possible before sealing. Poultry pieces may be frozen for 6 to 9 months.
- Frozen whole poultry purchased in tightly wrapped, heavy-duty plastic vacuum bags may be frozen as is for up to 1 year and do not need to be rewrapped.

Defrosting directives

NEVER defrost poultry at room temperature. Use the following methods and tips:

- **Refrigerator Method (recommended):** Good for poultry pieces and whole poultry. Place poultry on a tray in the fridge to prevent thawing juices from cross-contaminating other items and allow 5 hours per pound (10 hours per kilogram).
- **Cold Water Method:** Suitable for whole poultry purchased frozen in tightly wrapped, heavy-duty plastic. Submerge it in its original wrappings in cold water. Change the water every 30 minutes. Allow 1 hour per pound (2 hours per kilogram) to defrost.
- **Microwave Method:** If using the microwave for poultry pieces, remove the pieces closest to the edge of the plate as they thaw and cook the poultry immediately after defrosting.
- Make sure a whole bird is completely thawed before cooking or else the frozen meat closest to the bone will be undercooked, dramatically affecting the cooking time.

Cooking conventions

- Do NOT wash raw poultry before cooking as this can spread bacteria to kitchen surfaces.
- Use paper towels, not cloth, to wipe up any spilled poultry juices.
- Do not use the same utensils, dishes or cutting boards for raw and then cooked poultry.

- Wash hands, utensils and work surfaces with hot water and soap after handling or preparing poultry.
- Marinate poultry in the refrigerator for up to 2 days but never at room temperature.
- Make sure stuffing is completely cooled before inserting into the cavity.
- Stuff a whole bird JUST before cooking. Stuff no more than 2/3 full as the stuffing will expand during cooking.
- When basting, brush sauce on cooked surfaces only. Don't use a brush that has previously been in contact with raw poultry.
- Leftover marinade must be boiled for 5 to 7 minutes before basting or dipping. Better yet, set aside part of the marinade before you add it to the raw meat. Don't reuse marinades.
- Always cook poultry until done. Partial cooking can encourage bacterial growth.

Temperature tips

- At Practical Gourmet, we recommend using a digital instant-read thermometer or thermometer fork that gives a temperature reading, and not just a doneness range, to test for accurate, safe internal temperatures. Wash the device in hot, soapy water after use.
- To check that your thermometer is accurate, place it in boiling water and ensure it reaches 212°F (100°C).
- Insert the thermometer into the thickest part of the food, away from bone, fat or gristle, and hold it there for at least 30 seconds.

Temperature rules for safe doneness

- Ground chicken or turkey 175°F (80°C)
- Chicken or turkey pieces 170°F (77°C)
- Whole chicken (without stuffing) 180°F (82°C)
- Whole stuffed chicken (temperature 180°F (82°C) measured in meat)
- Stuffing cooked in poultry 165°F (74°C)

Leftovers

- Refrigerate leftovers within 2 hours, or 1 hour if the room temperature is more than 90°F (32°C).
- Remove any meat from the carcass immediately after the first meal and store it in the refrigerator in shallow containers so it can cool quickly.
- Boil the carcass for soup within 3 days or freeze it for up to 3 months.
- Use refrigerated poultry and stuffing within 3 days, and gravy within 1 to 2 days.
- Cooked poultry may be frozen for up to 3 months.

Chicken Samosas

These crisp pastries are filled with tender chicken and cooked vegetables. Good as is or dipped in sweet chili sauce, chutney, plum sauce or ketchup. To make ahead, prepare them to the baking stage, then wrap them individually in plastic wrap and freeze. Or you can bake them before freezing and reheat them in the microwave.

Olive oil	**1 tbsp.**	**15 mL**
Finely chopped onion	**2 cups**	**500 mL**
Ground chicken	**1 lb.**	**454 g**
Lemon pepper (optional)	**1/2 tsp.**	**2 mL**
Garlic cloves, minced	**2**	**2**
Diced peeled potato	**1/4 lb.**	**113 g**
Frozen peas	**2/3 cup**	**150 mL**
Low-sodium prepared chicken broth	**1/2 cup**	**125 mL**
Grated carrot	**1/3 cup**	**75 mL**
Garlic and herb no-salt seasoning	**1 1/2 tsp.**	**7 mL**
All-purpose flour	**2 tbsp.**	**30 mL**
Water	**3 tbsp.**	**45 mL**
Samosa wrappers (see Note)	**18**	**18**

For the filling, heat olive oil in a large saucepan on medium. Add onion and cook for 5 to 10 minutes, stirring often, until onion is soft and golden.

Add next 3 ingredients. Cook on medium for about 5 minutes, stirring constantly, until chicken is broken up and no pink remains.

Stir in next 5 ingredients and bring to a boil. Reduce heat to medium and cook, covered, for 15 to 20 minutes, stirring occasionally, until potato is tender. Remove cover. Increase heat, if necessary, to boil off any remaining moisture. Set aside to cool.

Stir flour into water in a small cup until it reaches consistency of smooth paste.

Lay 1 samosa wrapper on work surface (diagram 1). Fold according to diagrams 2 to 5, moistening edges of wrapper with flour mixture. Turn over. Spoon 3 tbsp. (45 mL) chicken filling into pocket. Moisten flaps with flour mixture (diagram 6). Fold to seal (diagram 7).

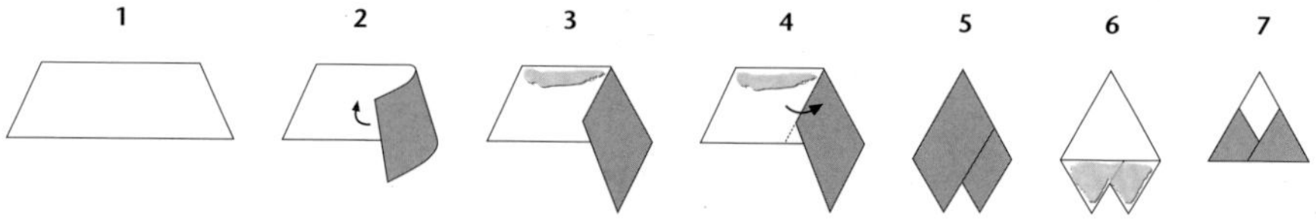

Arrange, seam-side down, on a greased baking sheet. Repeat with remaining wrappers, flour mixture and filling. Spray samosas lightly with cooking spray. Bake in 400°F (200°C) oven for about 15 minutes until crisp and lightly golden. Makes 18 samosas.

Note: Samosa wrappers can be found in the freezer sections of large grocery stores or East Indian markets.

1 samosa: *110 Calories; 4.5 g Total Fat (0.5 g Mono, 0 g Poly, 1.5 g Sat); 20 mg Cholesterol; 12 g Carbohydrate (0 g Fibre, 1 g Sugar); 6 g Protein; 95 mg Sodium*

Empanadas

Allow extra time to make these little finger foods—they're well worth it.

Butter (or hard margarine)	**1 tbsp.**	**15 mL**
Chopped onion	**1/2 cup**	**125 mL**
Ground chicken	**1/2 lb.**	**225 g**
All-purpose flour	**2 tbsp.**	**30 mL**
Milk	**1/2 cup**	**125 mL**
Chopped ripe olives	**3 tbsp.**	**45 mL**
Raisins, coarsely chopped	**1/4 cup**	**60 mL**
Worcestershire sauce	**1 tsp.**	**5 mL**
Garlic powder	**1/2 tsp.**	**2 mL**
Dried basil	**1/4 tsp.**	**1 mL**
Dried oregano	**1/4 tsp.**	**1 mL**
Black pepper	**1/8 tsp.**	**0.5 mL**
Hot pepper sauce	**1/8 tsp.**	**0.5 mL**
Salt	**1/8 tsp.**	**0.5 mL**

Pastry for 3 or 4 double crust pies

Heat butter in a medium frying pan over medium. Add onion and sauté until partially cooked.

Add chicken and scramble-fry until no pink remains.

Stir in flour. Stir in milk until mixture boils and thickens. Remove from heat.

Stir in next 9 ingredients.

Roll pastry. Cut into 3 inch (7.5 cm) rounds. Place 1 tsp. (5 mL) chicken mixture in centre of each round. Moisten half of outside edge with water. Fold over and press with a fork to seal. Cut slits in top. Arrange on an ungreased baking sheet. Bake in 400°F (200°C) oven for 15 to 20 minutes until browned. Serve hot. Makes 4 1/2 to 5 dozen empanadas.

1 empanada: *120 Calories; 8 g Total Fat (3.5 g Mono, 2 g Poly, 2 g Sat); 0 mg Cholesterol; 12 g Carbohydrate (0 g Fibre, 0 g Sugar); 2 g Protein; 135 mg Sodium*

Steamed Chicken Dumplings

These cute dumplings are packed with the pleasing Asian flavours of ginger, garlic and soy. Perfect dim sum fare with an appealing look.

Finely chopped water chestnuts	**2 tbsp.**	**30 mL**
Grated carrot	**1 tbsp.**	**15 mL**
Soy sauce	**4 tsp.**	**20 mL**
Finely chopped green onion	**1 tbsp.**	**15 mL**
Rice wine vinegar	**2 tsp.**	**10 mL**
Cornstarch	**1 tsp.**	**5 mL**
Finely grated ginger root (or 1/8 tsp., 0.5 mL, ground ginger)	**1/2 tsp.**	**2 mL**
Garlic clove, minced (or 1/4 tsp., 1 mL, powder)	**1**	**1**
Ground chicken	**1/2 lb.**	**225 g**
Round dumpling wrappers	**12**	**12**

Combine first 8 ingredients in a medium bowl.

Add chicken and mix well.

Arrange wrappers on a work surface. Place about 1 tbsp. (15 mL) chicken mixture in centre of each wrapper. Dampen edges with water. Gather up wrappers around filling, pinching to make small pleats, leaving top slightly open. Tap dumplings gently on work surface to flatten bottom slightly. Arrange dumplings, evenly spaced apart, in a greased 9 x 9 inch (23 x 23 cm) pan, being careful dumplings do not touch sides of pan. Place a wire rack in bottom of roasting pan. Pour water into roasting pan until about 1 inch (2.5 cm) deep. Bring to a boil on stovetop. Set baking pan on wire rack. Cook, covered, on medium for about 8 minutes until filling is no longer pink and internal temperature reaches 175°F (80°C). Makes 12 dumplings.

1 dumpling: *50 Calories; 2.5 g Total Fat (0 g Mono, 0 g Poly, 0 g Sat); 15 mg Cholesterol; 2 g Carbohydrate (0 g Fibre, 0 g Sugar); 4 g Protein; 140 mg Sodium*

Asian Chicken Salad Rolls

Fresh-tasting salad rolls are even better when they're stuffed with bean sprouts and cilantro. Served up with sweet chili sauce, these will disappear fast!

Rice vermicelli, broken up	**2 1/2 oz.**	**70 g**
Finely chopped cooked chicken (see Tip, below)	**3/4 cup**	**175 mL**
Shredded romaine lettuce, lightly packed	**1/2 cup**	**125 mL**
Grated carrot	**1/3 cup**	**75 mL**
Chopped fresh bean sprouts	**2 tbsp.**	**30 mL**
Chopped fresh cilantro (or parsley)	**2 tbsp.**	**30 mL**
Sesame oil (for flavour)	**1 tsp.**	**5 mL**
Salt	**1/8 tsp.**	**0.5 mL**
Rice paper rounds (6 inch, 15 cm, diameter)	**16**	**16**
Sweet chili sauce	**1/2 cup**	**125 mL**

Place vermicelli in a small heatproof bowl and cover with boiling water. Let stand for about 5 minutes until tender. Drain and rinse with cold water. Drain well. Transfer to a medium bowl.

Add next 7 ingredients and toss well.

Place 1 rice paper round in a shallow bowl of hot water until just softened. Place on a work surface. Spoon about 1/4 cup (60 mL) chicken mixture across centre. Fold sides over filling and roll up tightly from bottom to enclose filling. Transfer to a serving plate. Cover with a damp towel to prevent drying. Repeat with remaining rice paper rounds and chicken mixture.

Serve with chili sauce. Makes 16 rolls.

***1 roll with 1 1/2 tsp. (7 mL) chili sauce:** 90 Calories; 1 g Total Fat (0 g Mono, 0 g Poly, 0 g Sat); 10 mg Cholesterol; 16 g Carbohydrate (0 g Fibre, 3 g Sugar); 3 g Protein; 95 mg Sodium*

Tip: Don't have any leftover chicken? Start with 2 boneless, skinless chicken breast halves (about 4 oz., 113 g, each). Place them in a large frying pan with 1 cup (250 mL) water or chicken broth. Simmer, covered, for 12 to 14 minutes until no longer pink inside. Drain well and chop. Makes about 2 cups (500 mL) of cooked chicken.

Lettuce Wraps

For football games or playoff nights, this appetizer gets high scores. Hand out napkins and settle the bowl of filling on a plate surrounded by plenty of lettuce for visual appeal. Be prepared to cook up a second batch at intermission!

Cooking oil	**1 tsp.**	**5 mL**
Boneless, skinless chicken breast half (about 5 oz., 140 g), cut into 1/2 inch (12 mm) pieces	**1**	**1**
Grated carrot	**1/4 cup**	**60 mL**
Slivered onion	**1/4 cup**	**60 mL**
Slivered green pepper	**1 tbsp.**	**15 mL**
Slivered orange pepper	**1 tbsp.**	**15 mL**
Slivered red pepper	**1 tbsp.**	**15 mL**
Package of instant noodles (3 1/2 oz., 100 g) with chicken seasoning packet	**1**	**1**
Water	**1/4 cup**	**60 mL**
Unsalted peanuts	**1/4 cup**	**60 mL**
Hoisin sauce	**1 tbsp.**	**15 mL**
Liquid honey	**1 tsp.**	**5 mL**
Hot pepper sauce	**1/4 tsp.**	**1 mL**
Pepper	**1/8 tsp.**	**0.5 mL**
Chili powder, to taste		
Garlic powder, to taste		
Butter (or green leaf) lettuce leaves	**8**	**8**

Heat cooking oil in a large frying pan on medium. Add chicken and scramble-fry for 5 to 10 minutes until no longer pink.

Add next 5 ingredients and stir-fry until vegetables are tender-crisp.

Break noodles into 6 pieces. Set aside seasoning packet. Stir noodles and water into chicken mixture. Simmer, covered, for about 2 minutes until noodles are softened.

Add next 7 ingredients and half of seasoning packet. Cook, stirring, until heated through. Transfer to a small bowl.

Set bowl on a platter and surround with lettuce leaves. Spoon chicken mixture onto lettuce leaf and roll to enclose. Makes 8 wraps.

1 wrap: *110 Calories; 5 g Total Fat (2.5 g Mono, 1 g Poly, 1.5 g Sat); 10 mg Cholesterol; 12 g Carbohydrate (1 g Fibre, 2 g Sugar); 6 g Protein; 310 mg Sodium*

Onion Apple Phyllo Rolls

These appies are chic and dashing, tantalizing and tempting.

Butter (or hard margarine)	**2 tbsp.**	**30 mL**
Chopped onion	**2 cups**	**500 mL**
Grated peeled cooking apple (such as McIntosh)	**1 cup**	**250 mL**
Ground chicken	**1/2 lb.**	**225 g**
Grated Gruyère cheese	**2/3 cup**	**150 mL**
Chopped fresh thyme (or 1/2 tsp., 2 mL, dried)	**2 tsp.**	**10 mL**
Salt	**1/2 tsp.**	**2 mL**
Pepper	**1/4 tsp.**	**1 mL**
Phyllo pastry sheets, thawed according to package directions	**6**	**6**
Butter (or hard margarine), melted	**1/3 cup**	**75 mL**
Sesame seeds, toasted (see Tip, page 72)	**1 tbsp.**	**15 mL**

Melt first amount of butter in a large frying pan on medium. Add onion and cook for 5 to 10 minutes, stirring often, until softened.

Stir in apple. Reduce heat to medium-low. Cook for about 20 minutes, stirring occasionally, until onion is very soft and golden. Transfer to a medium bowl. Cool for 10 minutes.

Add next 5 ingredients. Mix well.

Lay pastry sheets on top of each other. Cut sheets in half crosswise, making 12 sheets. Place 1 sheet on a work surface with long side closest to you. Cover remaining sheets with a damp towel to prevent drying.

Brush sheet with melted butter and cut in half crosswise. Place about 1 tbsp. (15 mL) chicken mixture on lowest end of 1 half of sheet, about 1 inch (2.5 cm) from edge. Fold bottom edge of sheet over chicken mixture. Fold in sides. Roll up from bottom to enclose filling. Place seam side down on a greased baking sheet with sides. Cover with a separate damp towel. Repeat with remaining pastry sheets and chicken mixture. Brush tops of rolls with any remaining butter and sprinkle with sesame seeds. Bake in 400°F (200°C) oven for about 15 minutes until pastry is golden, chicken is no longer pink and internal temperature reaches 175°F (80°C). Makes 24 rolls.

***1 roll:** 90 Calories; 6 g Total Fat (1.5 g Mono, 0 g Poly, 3 g Sat); 20 mg Cholesterol; 4 g Carbohydrate (0 g Fibre, 0 g Sugar); 3 g Protein; 125 mg Sodium*

Chicken Satay with Peanut Sauce

Skewers of chicken satay have always been a favourite at Thai restaurants. Bring your guests a little of that authentic flavour paired with a delectable peanut sauce.

Boneless, skinless chicken breast halves	**1 lb.**	**454 g**
Sesame oil (for flavour)	**2 tbsp.**	**30 mL**
Paprika	**1/2 tsp.**	**2 mL**
Salt	**1 tsp.**	**5 mL**
Pepper	**1/2 tsp.**	**2 mL**
Bamboo skewers (8 inches, 20 cm, each), soaked in water for 10 minutes)	**12**	**12**
Sesame oil (for flavour)	**1/2 tsp.**	**2 mL**
Finely grated ginger root	**2 tsp.**	**10 mL**
Garlic cloves, minced (or 1/2 tsp., 2 mL, powder)	**2**	**2**
Peanut butter	**1/3 cup**	**75 mL**
Brown sugar, packed	**2 tbsp.**	**30 mL**
Lime juice	**2 tbsp.**	**30 mL**
Soy sauce	**2 tbsp.**	**30 mL**
Chili paste (sambal oelek)	**1/2 tsp.**	**2 mL**
Light coconut milk	**1/2 cup**	**125 mL**

Cut each chicken breast into 4 or 5 strips, about 1/2 inch (12 mm) wide. Put into a large resealable freezer bag. Combine next 4 ingredients in a small cup. Pour over chicken, seal bag and toss until chicken is well coated. Let stand in refrigerator for 1 to 2 hours, turning occasionally. Remove chicken and discard any remaining sesame oil mixture.

Thread chicken accordion-style onto skewers. Arrange on a baking sheet lined with greased foil. Bake in 350°F (175°C) oven for about 15 minutes, turning at halftime, until no longer pink inside.

For the peanut sauce heat sesame oil in a small saucepan on medium. Add ginger root and garlic. Cook, stirring, for about 1 minute until fragrant. Add next 5 ingredients. Cook, stirring, for about 5 minutes until peanut butter is melted.

Add coconut milk and cook, stirring, for about 1 minute until bubbling. Cool to room temperature. Serve with chicken skewers. Makes 12 skewers.

1 skewer with 4 tsp. (20 mL) sauce: *130 Calories; 7 g Total Fat (1 g Mono, 1 g Poly, 2 g Sat); 20 mg Cholesterol; 4 g Carbohydrate (0 g Fibre, 3 g Sugar); 11 g Protein; 410 mg Sodium*

Macadamia Chicken with Balsamic Orange Drizzle

Striking skewers to pique anyone's appetite—a unique combination of juicy orange, vibrant radicchio and chicken with a nutty crunch and bright, citrus flavours.

Orange juice	**1 cup**	**250 mL**
Liquid honey	**1 tbsp.**	**15 mL**
White balsamic vinegar	**1 tbsp.**	**15 mL**
Mayonnaise	**3 tbsp.**	**45 mL**
Plain yogurt	**3 tbsp.**	**45 mL**
Liquid honey	**1 tsp.**	**5 mL**
Grated orange zest (see Tip, page 52)	**1 tsp.**	**5 mL**
Boneless, skinless chicken breast halves (about 4 oz., 113 g, each), cut into 1 inch (2.5 cm) pieces	**2**	**2**
All-purpose flour	**1/4 cup**	**60 mL**
Finely chopped salted macadamia nuts	**1 cup**	**250 mL**
Radicchio leaves, cut into 1 inch (2.5 cm) strips	**3**	**3**
Small orange segments	**16**	**16**
Bamboo skewers (6 inches, 15 cm, each)	**16**	**16**

Bring first 3 ingredients to a boil in a small saucepan, stirring occasionally. Reduce heat to medium and gently boil for 15 minutes until thickened to a syrup consistency. Set aside to cool.

Combine next 4 ingredients in a shallow bowl.

Toss chicken in flour and roll each piece in mayonnaise mixture. Press into macadamia nuts until coated. Arrange on a greased baking sheet and spray chicken with cooking spray. Cook in 450°F (230°C) oven for 5 minutes until no longer pink inside.

Thread chicken, radicchio and orange segments, in order given, on skewers. Arrange on a serving plate and drizzle with orange juice mixture. Makes 16 skewers.

1 skewer: *120 Calories; 9 g Total Fat (6 g Mono, 1 g Poly, 1.5 g Sat); 10 mg Cholesterol; 7 g Carbohydrate (1 g Fibre, 3 g Sugar); 5 g Protein; 30 mg Sodium*

Chicken Saltimbocca Spikes

Full Italian flavours of fresh sage and prosciutto heighten the senses, and Marsala's fortified sweetness is the perfect complement. To make an inventive stand for your skewers, simply cut a lemon in half length wise, place it cut side down on a plate and securely lodge the skewers in the lemon.

Finely chopped fresh sage	**2 tbsp.**	**30 mL**
Pepper	**1/8 tsp.**	**0.5 mL**
Chicken breast fillets, cut crosswise into 3 pieces	**1/2 lbs.**	**225 g**
Prosciutto ham slices, cut lengthwise into 1 inch (2.5 cm) wide strips	**3 oz.**	**85 g**
Fresh sage leaves	**8**	**8**
Butter, melted	**2 tbsp.**	**30 mL**
Extra-virgin olive oil	**1 tbsp.**	**15 mL**
Marsala wine	**2 tbsp.**	**30 mL**
Bamboo cocktail picks or skewers, approximately	**18**	**18**
Lemon juice	**2 tbsp.**	**30 mL**

Sprinkle sage and pepper on chicken. Roll 1 prociutto strip around each chicken piece. Place, seam side down, in a baking dish.

Scatter sage leaves over rolls. Drizzle with butter and olive oil. Bake in a 450°F (230°C) oven for 4 minutes. Drizzle with marsala. Bake for about 4 minutes until internal temperature reaches 175°F (80°C).

Skewer rolls. Drizzle with lemon juice and pan juices. Makes about 18 spikes.

1 spike: *45 Calories; 3 g Total Fat (1 g Mono, 0 g Poly, 1 g Sat); 15 mg Cholesterol; 0 g Carbohydrate (0 g Fibre, 0 g Sugar); 4 g Protein; 105 mg Sodium*

Buffalo Wings

Decide if you want hot wings or "suicide hot" wings, then cut the heat with your favourite blue cheese dip.

Large eggs, fork-beaten	**2**	**2**
Milk	**1/4 cup**	**60 mL**
Hot pepper sauce	**1 tbsp.**	**15 mL**
All-purpose flour	**2/3 cup**	**150 mL**
Seasoned salt	**2 tsp.**	**10 mL**
Pepper	**1/2 tsp.**	**2 mL**
Whole chicken wings (or drumettes)	**3 lbs.**	**1.4 kg**
Cooking oil, for deep-frying		
Commercial Louisiana Hot Sauce	**4 tbsp.**	**60 mL**
Butter, melted	**3 tbsp.**	**45 mL**

Combine eggs, milk and hot pepper sauce in a small bowl.

Combine flour, seasoned salt and pepper in a separate small bowl.

Remove wing tips and discard. Cut wings apart at joint. Dip a few pieces into egg mixture then into flour mixture to coat. Deep-fry in hot 375°F (190°C) cooking oil for 8 to 10 minutes until browned and crisp. Drain on paper towels. Put cooked chicken into a large pail or bowl with a cover.

Combine hot sauce and butter in a small bowl. Drizzle cooked chicken with hot sauce. Cover and shake for 1 to 2 minutes to distribute sauce evenly. Makes about 36 wing pieces or 24 drumettes.

1 wing piece: *110 Calories; 6 g Total Fat (2.5 g Mono, 1.5 g Poly, 1 g Sat); 40 mg Cholesterol; 2 g Carbohydrate (0 g Fibre, 0 g Sugar); 11 g Protein; 200 mg Sodium*

Bourbon Chicken Wings

Your favourite barbecue sauce is given added dimension with the heady richness of bourbon and the satisfying sweetness of orange juice and honey. Guests will happily hover around—and quickly devour—a basket of these tasty wings. Pile the wings high on a plate or in a parchment paper-lined basket. Have finger bowls with water and a slice of orange at the ready.

Barbecue sauce (see Tip, below)	**1 cup**	**250 mL**
Bourbon	**1/2 cup**	**125 mL**
Frozen concentrated orange juice	**1/4 cup**	**60 mL**
Liquid honey	**1/4 cup**	**60 mL**
Seasoned salt	**1 tsp.**	**5 mL**
Split chicken wings, tips discarded	**3 lbs.**	**1.4 kg**

Combine first 5 ingredients, reserving 1/2 cup (125 mL).

Pour remaining barbecue sauce mixture into a large resealable freezer bag. Add chicken wings and chill for 2 hours. Drain and discard marinade. Grill wings on direct medium-low heat for about 15 minutes per side until no longer pink at the bone. Brush with reserved barbecue sauce mixture during final 10 minutes of cooking. Makes 30 to 35 wings.

***1 wing:** 140 Calories; 8 g Total Fat (3 g Mono, 1.5 g Poly, 2 g Sat); 40 mg Cholesterol; 5 g Carbohydrate (0 g Fibre, 3 g Sugar); 9 g Protein; 180 mg Sodium*

Tip: Try for different shades of flavour by using a smoky barbecue sauce one time and a hot and spicy one the next.

Stuffed Mushrooms

These tasty little tidbits can be made a few hours ahead, then broiled when you need them.

Medium mushrooms	**24**	**24**
Butter (or hard margarine)	**3 tbsp.**	**45 mL**
Finely chopped onion	**1/2 cup**	**125 mL**
Finely chopped celery	**3 tbsp.**	**45 mL**
Cooked ground chicken	**1/2 cup**	**125 mL**
Dry bread crumbs	**1/4 cup**	**60 mL**
Sour cream	**1/4 cup**	**60 mL**
Poultry seasoning	**1/4 tsp.**	**1 mL**
Dried basil	**1/4 tsp.**	**1 mL**
Dried oregano	**1/4 tsp.**	**1 mL**
Garlic powder	**1/4 tsp.**	**1 mL**
Salt	**1/4 tsp.**	**1 mL**
Pepper	**1/4 tsp.**	**1 mL**
Grated Parmesan cheese	**2 tbsp.**	**30 mL**

Gently twist stems from mushrooms. Chop stems and set aside.

Melt butter in a large frying pan on medium. Add onion, celery and mushroom stems and sauté until soft.

Add next 9 ingredients and stir well. Stuff mushrooms with mixture.

Dip tops in cheese and arrange on a baking sheet. Broil on second rack from top for 3 to 5 minutes or bake in 350°F (175°C) oven for 10 to 15 minutes until crusty. Makes 24 stuffed mushrooms.

1 stuffed mushroom: *30 Calories; 2 g Total Fat (0.5 g Mono, 0 g Poly, 1 g Sat); 5 mg Cholesterol; 2 g Carbohydrate (0 g Fibre, 0 g Sugar); 2 g Protein; 55 mg Sodium*

Summer Spinach Salad

This fresh, colourful blend includes sweet summer berries, sharp Asiago, vibrant pistachios and beautifully grilled chicken—truly a light and easy meal salad to enjoy on the patio.

Boneless, skinless chicken breast halves	**1 lb.**	**454 g**
Salt	**1/4 tsp.**	**1 mL**
Pepper	**1/4 tsp.**	**1 mL**
Fresh spinach leaves, lightly packed	**6 cups**	**1.5 L**
Fresh blueberries	**1/2 cup**	**125 mL**
Fresh raspberries	**1/2 cup**	**125 mL**
Thinly sliced red onion	**1/2 cup**	**125 mL**
Grated Asiago cheese	**1/4 cup**	**60 mL**
Pistachios	**1/4 cup**	**60 mL**
Lemon juice	**3 tbsp.**	**45 mL**
Olive (or cooking) oil	**3 tbsp.**	**45 mL**
Dijon mustard	**2 tsp.**	**10 mL**
Liquid honey	**2 tsp.**	**10 mL**
Grated lemon zest (see Tip, page 52)	**1 tsp.**	**5 mL**
Garlic clove, minced (or 1/4 tsp., 1 mL, powder)	**1**	**1**
Salt	**1/4 tsp.**	**1 mL**

Sprinkle both sides of chicken with salt and pepper. Preheat gas barbecue to medium. Cook chicken on a greased grill for about 7 minutes per side until internal temperature reaches 170°F (77°C). Transfer to a cutting board to cool. Cut into 1/2 inch (12 mm) slices. Transfer to a large bowl.

Stir in next 6 ingredients.

Whisk remaining 7 ingredients in a small bowl. Drizzle over spinach mixture and toss gently. Makes about 9 cups (2.25 L).

1 cup (250 mL): *150 Calories; 8 g Total Fat (4.5 g Mono, 1 g Poly, 1.5 g Sat); 30 mg Cholesterol; 6 g Carbohydrate (2 g Fibre, 3 g Sugar); 14 g Protein; 230 mg Sodium*

Blackened Chicken Caesar Salad

Blackened cooking originated in New Orleans. Traditionally, meat or fish is rubbed with Cajun spices and then cooked quickly in a hot, greased pan, giving the meat a crisp, dark crust. To speed things up, we've added the spices during cooking, with equally tasty results.

Grated Parmesan cheese	**1/2 cup**	**125 mL**
Cooking oil	**3 tbsp.**	**45 mL**
Sour cream	**3 tbsp.**	**45 mL**
White wine vinegar	**1 tbsp.**	**15 mL**
Lemon juice	**1 tsp.**	**5 mL**
Worcestershire sauce	**1 tsp.**	**5 mL**
Garlic salt	**1/2 tsp.**	**2 mL**
Pepper	**1/4 tsp.**	**1 mL**
Cooking oil	**1 tbsp.**	**15 mL**
Boneless, skinless chicken breast halves, cut into 3/4 inch (2 cm) pieces	**2 lbs.**	**900 g**
Ketchup	**2 tbsp.**	**30 mL**
Paprika	**1 tbsp.**	**15 mL**
Cayenne pepper	**1/2 tsp.**	**2 mL**
Chili powder	**1/2 tsp.**	**2 mL**
Ground thyme	**1/2 tsp.**	**2 mL**
Onion powder	**1/2 tsp.**	**2 mL**
Salt	**2 tsp.**	**10 mL**
Pepper	**1/2 tsp.**	**2 mL**
Heads of romaine lettuce, cut or torn	**2**	**2**
Croutons	**1 cup**	**250 mL**
Grated Parmesan cheese	**1/4 cup**	**60 mL**
Grated Parmesan cheese, for garnish		

For the dressing, combine first 8 ingredients in a small bowl. Chill, covered, for 10 minutes to blend flavours.

For the chicken, heat a wok or large frying pan on medium-high until very hot. Add cooking oil. Add chicken and stir-fry for 6 to 7 minutes until chicken is lightly browned.

Add next 8 ingredients. Stir-fry for 8 to 10 minutes until chicken is no longer pink. Remove from heat.

Combine next 3 ingredients in a large bowl. Drizzle with dressing and toss gently. Arrange on 8 dinner plates. Scatter chicken mixture over top. Garnish with second amount of cheese. Makes 8 servings.

***1 serving:** 290 Calories; 13 g Total Fat (6 g Mono, 2.5 g Poly, 3.5 g Sat); 75 mg Cholesterol; 11 g Carbohydrate (4 g Fibre, 3 g Sugar); 33 g Protein; 1010 mg Sodium*

Chicken Taco Layers

This easy layered salad will be a sure hit. It features everyone's favourite Mexican flavours, all dressed in a delicious lime and sour cream blend.

Shredded iceberg lettuce, lightly packed	**4 cups**	**1 L**
Chopped cooked chicken (see Tip, page 14)	**2 cups**	**500 mL**
Medium salsa	**1/2 cup**	**125 mL**
Chopped avocado	**2 cups**	**500 mL**
Chopped tomato	**2 cups**	**500 mL**
Chopped green onion	**3/4 cup**	**175 mL**
Grated Mexican cheese blend	**1 cup**	**250 mL**
Sour cream	**1/2 cup**	**125 mL**
Chopped fresh jalapeño peppers (see Tip, page 58)	**2 tbsp.**	**30 mL**
Lime juice	**2 tbsp.**	**30 mL**
Chopped fresh cilantro (or parsley)	**1 tbsp.**	**15 mL**
Olive (or cooking) oil	**1 tbsp.**	**15 mL**
Salt	**1/2 tsp.**	**2 mL**
Crushed tortilla chips	**1 cup**	**250 mL**

Arrange lettuce in an extra-large glass bowl.

Combine chicken and salsa in a medium bowl. Spoon over lettuce.

Layer next 4 ingredients, in order given, over chicken mixture.

Process next 6 ingredients in a blender until smooth. Drizzle over cheese.

Scatter tortilla chips over top. Makes about 13 cups (3.25 L).

1 1/2 cups (375 mL): *230 Calories; 16 g Total Fat (7 g Mono, 1.5 g Poly, 6 g Sat); 45 mg Cholesterol; 10 g Carbohydrate (4 g Fibre, 3 g Sugar); 14 g Protein; 370 mg Sodium*

Grilled Chicken and Artichoke Salad

A colourful, tangy salad that's perfect for company.

Olive (or cooking) oil	**1/3 cup**	**75 mL**
Balsamic vinegar	**1/4 cup**	**60 mL**
Liquid honey	**2 tbsp.**	**30 mL**
Chopped fresh basil (or 3/4 tsp., 4 mL, dried)	**1 tbsp.**	**15 mL**
Garlic cloves, minced (or 1/2 tsp., 2 mL, powder)	**2**	**2**
Lemon pepper	**1 tsp.**	**5 mL**
Boneless, skinless chicken breast halves	**3/4 lb.**	**340 g**
Large red onion, cut into 8 wedges	**1**	**1**
Bag of fresh spinach (6 oz., 170 g), stems removed	**1**	**1**
Can of artichoke hearts (14 oz., 398 mL), drained and coarsely chopped	**1**	**1**
Halved cherry tomatoes	**1 cup**	**250 mL**
Chopped walnuts, toasted (see Tip, page 72)	**1 cup**	**250 mL**
Crumbled feta cheese (about 4 oz., 113 g)	**3/4 cup**	**175 mL**

For the marinade, combine first 6 ingredients in a jar with a tight-fitting lid. Shake well.

Place chicken in a large resealable freezer bag. Pour 1/2 of marinade over top. Seal bag and turn unti chicken is coated. Marinate in refrigerator for 3 hours. Drain and discard marinade. Preheat barbecue to medium. Cook chicken on a greased grill for about 5 minutes per side until no longer pink inside. Chop coarsely and transfer to a large bowl.

Cook onion on greased grill for about 10 minutes, turning once, until softened and grill marks appear. Add to chicken.

Add remaining 5 ingredients and toss lightly. Drizzle with remaining marinade and toss well. Makes 6 servings.

1 serving: *330 Calories; 26 g Total Fat (9 g Mono, 10 g Poly, 5 g Sat); 35 mg Cholesterol; 12 g Carbohydrate (5 g Fibre, 5 g Sugar); 15 g Protein; 500 mg Sodium*

Cobb Salad with Honey Vinaigrette

The great things about this salad are that it looks great, 90 percent of the work can be done ahead of time to wow your guests, and it showcases some great local products. See what is available at the market—maybe fresh beets, baby carrots, baby sweet onions. We've suggested three types of common garden lettuce here, but use whatever you've got on hand. The point is to have a variety of greens.

Head of iceberg lettuce	**1/2**	**1/2**
Head of romaine lettuce	**1/2**	**1/2**
Head of butter leaf lettuce	**1**	**1**
Tomatoes, diced	**2**	**2**
Chopped cooked chicken (see Tip, page 14)	**2 cups**	**500 mL**
Cooked, crumbled bacon (8 slices)	**1 cup**	**250 mL**
Hard-boiled eggs, peeled and sliced	**4**	**4**
Crumbled blue cheese or your favourite cheese	**1 cup**	**250 mL**
Blanched green peas (see Tip, below)	**1 cup**	**250 mL**
Chopped chives or green onions	**1/2 cup**	**125 mL**
Red wine vinegar	**1/4 cup**	**60 mL**
Liquid honey	**1 tsp.**	**5 mL**
Juice from 1/2 lemon		
Worcestershire sauce	**1 tsp.**	**5 mL**
Dijon mustard	**1 tbsp.**	**15 mL**
Finely diced onion	**1/4 cup**	**60 mL**
Salt	**1/2 tsp.**	**2 mL**
Pepper	**1/4 tsp.**	**1 mL**
Canola oil	**1 cup**	**250 mL**

Wash lettuces well and tear into large pieces. Toss lettuces together and arrange on a large platter. Arrange next 7 ingredients in rows over top. Set aside.

Add remaining 9 ingredients in a jar with a tight-fitting lid and shake well. Drizzle over salad and serve immediately. Makes 7 servings.

***1 serving:** 500 Calories; 41 g Total Fat (21 g Mono, 9 g Poly, 8 g Sat); 160 mg Cholesterol; 11 g Carbohydrate (4 g Fibre, 5 g Sugar); 23 g Protein; 600 mg Sodium*

Tip: Blanch peas by placing them into a saucepan of boiling water. Have a bowl of ice water at the ready, and when the peas have cooked for 2 minutes, drain them and put them into the ice water to chill and stop the cooking process.

Chicken Fajita Pasta Salad

This hearty penne salad packs all the flavour of your favourite fajitas with chili heat, barbecued chicken and sautéed veggies.

Water	**8 cups**	**2 L**
Salt	**1 tsp.**	**5 mL**
Penne pasta	**2 cups**	**500 mL**
Boneless, skinless chicken breast halves	**3/4 lb.**	**340 g**
Salsa	**2 tbsp.**	**30 mL**
Cooking oil	**1 tbsp.**	**15 mL**
Ground cumin	**1 tsp.**	**5 mL**
Dried crushed chilies	**1/4 tsp.**	**1 mL**
Thinly sliced green pepper	**1 cup**	**250 mL**
Thinly sliced onion	**1 cup**	**250 mL**
Thinly sliced red pepper	**1 cup**	**250 mL**
Frozen kernel corn	**1/2 cup**	**125 mL**
Salsa	**1/4 cup**	**60 mL**
Sour cream	**1/4 cup**	**60 mL**
Lime juice	**2 tsp.**	**10 mL**
Salt	**1/4 tsp.**	**1 mL**
Thinly sliced green onion	**3 tbsp.**	**45 mL**

Combine water and salt in a large saucepan and bring to a boil. Add pasta and cook, uncovered, for 14 to 16 minutes, stirring occasionally, until tender but firm. Drain. Rinse with cold water and drain well. Transfer to a large bowl.

Brush both sides of chicken breasts with salsa. Arrange on a greased baking sheet with sides. Bake in 375°F (190°C) oven for about 9 minutes per side until internal temperature reaches 170°F (77°C). Transfer to a cutting board and let stand until cool. Slice thinly. Add to pasta.

Heat cooking oil in a large frying pan on medium. Add cumin and chilies and cook, stirring, for about 1 minute until fragrant. Add next 4 ingredients. Cook for about 10 minutes, stirring occasionally, until vegetables are softened. Set aside to cool. Add to pasta mixture.

Combine next 4 ingredients in a small bowl. Add to pasta mixture and toss well. Sprinkle with green onion. Makes about 8 cups (2 L).

1 cup (250 mL): *220 Calories; 4.5 g Total Fat (1.5 g Mono, 0.5 g Poly, 1 g Sat); 30 mg Cholesterol; 30 g Carbohydrate (2 g Fibre, 3 g Sugar); 14 g Protein; 260 mg Sodium*

Spinach Orzo Salad

The complaints about eating leftover chicken will soon cease when your family tastes this light and fresh salad. This colourful spinach creation contains orzo, a tiny pasta similar in shape to rice.

Water	**2 cups**	**500 mL**
Salt	**1/4 tsp.**	**1 mL**
Orzo	**1/2 cup**	**125 mL**
Fresh spinach leaves, lightly packed	**4 cups**	**1 L**
Chopped cooked chicken (see Tip, page 14)	**2 cups**	**500 mL**
Diced fresh tomato	**1 1/2 cups**	**375 mL**
Kalamata olives, chopped	**1/2 cup**	**125 mL**
Crumbled feta cheese	**1/3 cup**	**75 mL**
Olive (or cooking) oil	**1/4 cup**	**60 mL**
Balsamic vinegar	**2 tbsp.**	**30 mL**
Lemon juice	**1 tbsp.**	**15 mL**
Chopped fresh oregano (or 1/4 tsp., 1 mL, dried)	**1 tsp.**	**5 mL**
Salt	**1/4 tsp.**	**1 mL**
Pepper	**1 tsp.**	**5 mL**

Combine water and salt in a small saucepan. Bring to a boil. Add orzo. Boil, uncovered, for about 8 minutes, stirring occasionally, until tender but firm. Drain. Rinse with cold water. Drain well. Transfer to a large bowl.

Add next 4 ingredients and toss well.

For the dressing, process remaining 7 ingredients in a blender until smooth. Drizzle over salad and toss well. Makes about 8 1/2 cups (2.1 L).

1 cup (250 mL): *190 Calories; 12 g Total Fat (7 g Mono, 1.5 g Poly, 2.5 g Sat); 30 mg Cholesterol; 11 g Carbohydrate (1 g Fibre, 2 g Sugar); 10 g Protein; 340 mg Sodium*

Pulled Tex Chicken

Got a hankerin' for some good, old southwestern sandwich flavour? Then this is the meal for you! Sweet and tangy with an authentic flavour. Tastes even better when topped with your favourite coleslaw. Don't forget the napkins!

Sliced onion	**1 1/2 cups**	**375 mL**
Barbecue sauce	**1 cup**	**250 mL**
Can of tomato sauce (7 1/2 oz., 213 mL)	**1**	**1**
Can of diced green chilies (4 oz., 113 g)	**1**	**1**
Chili powder	**1 tbsp.**	**15 mL**
Dried oregano	**1 tsp.**	**5 mL**
Ground cumin	**1/2 tsp.**	**2 mL**
Ground cinnamon	**1/4 tsp.**	**1 mL**
Boneless, skinless chicken thighs	**1 3/4 lbs.**	**790 g**
Crusty rolls	**6**	**6**

Combine first 8 ingredients in a 3 1/2 to 4 quart (3.5 to 4 L) slow cooker.

Add chicken. Spoon barbecue sauce mixture over chicken to cover. Cook, covered, on Low for 7 to 8 hours or on High for 3 1/2 to 4 hours until chicken is tender. Remove chicken to a cutting board using tongs. Shred chicken using 2 forks. Add to sauce mixture and stir.

Serve chicken mixture in rolls. Makes 6 sandwiches.

1 sandwich: *370 Calories; 9 g Total Fat (1.5 g Mono, 1.5 g Poly, 2 g Sat); 110 mg Cholesterol; 43 g Carbohydrate (3 g Fibre, 6 g Sugar); 32 g Protein; 1170 mg Sodium*

Grilled Quesadillas

Crispy and golden on the outside with a spicy chicken filling on the inside.

Sour cream	**1/3 cup**	**75 mL**
Chili sauce	**2 tbsp.**	**30 mL**
Chopped cooked chicken (see Tip, page 14)	**3 cups**	**750 mL**
Grated Monterey Jack cheese	**1 2/3 cups**	**400 mL**
Flour tortillas (10 inch, 25 cm, diameter)	**4**	**4**
Sliced pickled jalapeño peppers	**1 tbsp.**	**15 mL**
Medium tomatoes, seeds removed, diced	**2**	**2**
Finely chopped green onion	**3 tbsp.**	**45 mL**
Chopped fresh parsley (or 1 1/2 tsp., 7 mL, flakes)	**2 tbsp.**	**30 mL**
Cooking oil	**1 tbsp.**	**15 mL**

Combine sour cream and chili sauce in a medium bowl. Add chicken and toss until coated.

Divide and scatter cheese over 1/2 of each tortilla. Divide and spoon chicken mixture evenly over cheese.

Layer next 4 ingredients over chicken mixture. Fold each tortilla in half to enclose filling.

Preheat barbecue to medium. Brush tops of folded tortillas with 1/2 of cooking oil. Cook quesadillas, top side down, on a greased grill for 5 minutes. Brush with remaining cooking oil. Turn. Cook for about 5 minutes until crisp and golden and cheese is melted. Cut in 4 pieces to serve. Makes 4 servings.

***1 serving:** 710 Calories; 35 g Total Fat (9 g Mono, 3.5 g Poly, 15 g Sat); 150 mg Cholesterol; 47 g Carbohydrate (3 g Fibre, 3 g Sugar); 49 g Protein; 920 mg Sodium*

Portobello Chicken Burger

Can't decide whether to make chicken or a portobello mushroom burgers? Have both at the same time! This makes a great alternative to a traditional beef burger.

Portobello mushrooms (about 6 oz., 170 g, each), stems and gills removed (see Note)	**4**	**4**
Olive (or canola) oil	**1 tbsp.**	**15 mL**
Salt, sprinkle		
Pepper, sprinkle		
Large egg, fork-beaten	**1**	**1**
Grated Parmesan cheese	**1/4 cup**	**60 mL**
Fine dry bread crumbs	**2 tbsp.**	**30 mL**
Sun-dried tomato pesto	**2 tbsp.**	**30 mL**
Finely chopped fresh rosemary	**1/4 tsp.**	**1 mL**
Salt	**1/4 tsp.**	**1 mL**
Pepper	**1/4 tsp.**	**1 mL**
Ground chicken	**3/4 lb.**	**340 g**
Whole wheat kaiser rolls, split	**4**	**4**
Mayonnaise	**1/4 cup**	**60 mL**
Romaine lettuce leaves	**4**	**4**

Brush mushrooms with olive oil and sprinkle with salt and pepper. Preheat barbecue to medium. Place mushrooms, stem side down, on an ungreased grill. Close lid and cook for about 5 minutes until grill marks appear. Transfer, stem side up, to a large plate.

Combine next 7 ingredients in a medium bowl. Add chicken and mix well. Divide into 4 equal portions. Shape into 4 1/2 inch (11 cm) patties. Press patties firmly into mushrooms. Place on a greased grill, patty side down. Close lid and cook for about 8 minutes until internal temperature of patty reaches 175°F (80°C). Turn. Close lid and cook for about 3 minutes until mushroom is tender and browned.

Place roll halves on a greased grill. Cook for about 1 minute until golden. Spread mayonnaise on roll halves. Serve patties, topped with lettuce, in rolls. Makes 4 burgers.

1 burger: *560 Calories; 32 g Total Fat (10 g Mono, 4 g Poly, 4 g Sat); 130 mg Cholesterol; 39 g Carbohydrate (5 g Fibre, 4 g Sugar); 29 g Protein; 880 mg Sodium*

Note: Because the gills can sometimes be bitter, be sure to remove them from the portobellos before stuffing. First remove the stems, then, using a small spoon, scrape out and discard the gills.

Pepper Lime Burgers

This zippy lime sauce brings summer to your senses, even when snow is in the forecast. If it's too cold to barbecue, broil the patties on a greased pan for about five minutes per side until the internal temperature reaches 175°F (80°C).

Light ranch dressing	**1/2 cup**	**125 mL**
Lime juice	**2 tbsp.**	**30 mL**
Grated lime zest (see Tip, below)	**1 tsp.**	**5 mL**
Pepper	**1/4 tsp.**	**1 mL**
Large egg, fork-beaten	**1**	**1**
Quick-cooking rolled oats	**3/4 cup**	**175 mL**
Garlic clove, minced (or 1/4 tsp., 1 mL, powder)	**1**	**1**
Ground chicken	**1 1/2 lbs.**	**680 g**
Whole wheat hamburger buns, split	**6**	**6**
Roasted red pepper pieces, drained and blotted dry	**6**	**6**
Green leaf lettuce leaves, halved	**3**	**3**

For the ranch lime sauce, combine first 4 ingredients in a small bowl.

Preheat gas barbecue to medium. Combine next 4 ingredients and 1/4 cup (60 mL) ranch lime sauce in a medium bowl. Add chicken and mix well. Divide into 6 equal portions. Shape into 1/2 inch (12 mm) thick patties. Cook on a greased grill for about 5 minutes per side until fully cooked and internal temperature reaches 175°F (80°C).

Spread remaining Ranch Lime Sauce on bottom halves of buns. Layer patties, roasted red pepper and lettuce over sauce. Cover with top halves of buns. Makes 6 burgers.

***1 burger:** 440 Calories; 22 g Total Fat (1 g Mono, 1 g Poly, 1 g Sat); 120 mg Cholesterol; 32 g Carbohydrate (3 g Fibre, 5 g Sugar); 27 g Protein; 710 mg Sodium*

Tip: When a recipe calls for grated zest and juice, it's easier to grate the fruit first, then juice it. Be careful not to grate down to the pith (the white part of the peel), which is bitter and is best avoided.

Greek Chicken Wrap

Moist chicken thigh meat combines with classic Greek flavours in a wrap fit to feed company.

Lemon juice	**2 tbsp.**	**30 mL**
Olive (or cooking) oil	**2 tbsp.**	**30 mL**
Dried oregano	**1/2 tsp.**	**2 mL**
Garlic clove, minced (or 1/4 tsp., 1 mL, powder)	**1**	**1**
Salt	**1/4 tsp.**	**1 mL**
Pepper	**1/4 tsp.**	**1 mL**
Boneless, skinless chicken thighs, halved	**3/4 lb.**	**340 g**
Chopped green pepper	**1/2 cup**	**125 mL**
Chopped tomato	**1/2 cup**	**125 mL**
Crumbled feta cheese	**1/4 cup**	**60 mL**
Finely chopped English cucumber (with peel)	**1/4 cup**	**60 mL**
Plain yogurt	**1/4 cup**	**60 mL**
Finely chopped onion	**2 tbsp.**	**30 mL**
Flour tortillas (9 inch, 23 cm, diameter)	**4**	**4**

Combine first 6 ingredients in a small cup.

Place chicken in a medium bowl. Add 2 tbsp. (30 mL) lemon juice mixture and stir until coated. Arrange on a greased baking sheet with sides. Cook in 375°F (190°C) oven for about 7 minutes per side until internal temperature reaches 165°F (74°C). Transfer to a cutting board and let stand for about 5 minutes, until cool enough to handle, before chopping.

Meanwhile, combine next 6 ingredients in a small bowl. Stir in remaining lemon mixture. Add chicken and stir well.

Spoon chicken mixture across centre of each tortilla. Fold sides over filling. Roll up from bottom to enclose. Makes 4 wraps.

1 wrap: *370 Calories; 16 g Total Fat (8 g Mono, 2 g Poly, 4.5 g Sat); 80 mg Cholesterol; 32 g Carbohydrate (2 g Fibre, 3 g Sugar); 23 g Protein; 570 mg Sodium*

Chicken and Ham Stack

One giant sandwich stacked with enough chicken, ham and vegetables to serve 6! For easier cutting, secure sandwich in 6 places with long picks before cutting into wedges. Looks colossal, tastes colossal!

Herb focaccia bread (10 inch, 25 cm, diameter)	**1**	**1**
Olive oil	**2 tsp.**	**10 mL**
Dijon mustard	**3 tbsp.**	**45 mL**
Liquid honey	**2 tbsp.**	**30 mL**
Light mayonnaise	**1 tbsp.**	**15 mL**
Finely chopped fresh rosemary (or 1/8 tsp., 0.5 mL, dried, crushed)	**1/2 tsp.**	**2 mL**
Romaine lettuce leaves	**4**	**4**
Thin slices of yellow pepper	**8**	**8**
Thin slices of tomato	**6**	**6**
Deli ham slices (about 4 1/2 oz., 125 g)	**5**	**5**
Sliced cooked chicken breast (about 2 small chicken breast halves) (see Tip, page 14)	**1 1/4 cups**	**300 mL**

Preheat broiler. Cut focaccia bread in half horizontally and brush cut sides with olive oil. Place, cut side up, on an ungreased baking sheet. Broil on top rack in oven for about 2 minutes until golden. Transfer to a cutting surface.

For the sweet mustard mayo, combine next 4 ingredients in a small bowl. Spread on toasted focaccia.

Place lettuce leaves on bottom half of focaccia. Layer remaining 4 ingredients, in order given, over lettuce. Cover with top half of focaccia. Cuts into 6 wedges.

***1 wedge:** 370 Calories; 10 g Total Fat (2 g Mono, 1 g Poly, 1.5 g Sat); 40 mg Cholesterol; 53 g Carbohydrate (2 g Fibre, 8 g Sugar); 20 g Protein; 810 mg Sodium*

Mango Salsa Chicken

Refreshing, delicious and pretty to look at! Spicy citrus and mango salsa is the perfect match for tender chicken. The salsa also goes well with salads, wraps, quesadillas and grilled fish.

Boneless, skinless chicken breast halves (about 4 oz., 113 g, each)	**4**	**4**
Olive oil	**2 tbsp.**	**30 mL**
Lime juice	**1 1/2 tbsp.**	**22 mL**
Grated lime zest (see Tip, page 52)	**1 1/2 tsp.**	**7 mL**
Cajun seasoning	**1 tsp.**	**5 mL**
Chopped frozen mango, thawed (see Note)	**1 cup**	**250 mL**
Finely diced red onion	**1/4 cup**	**60 mL**
Garlic clove, minced (or 1/4 tsp., 1 mL, powder)	**1**	**1**
Finely diced jalapeño pepper (see Tip, below)	**2 tbsp.**	**30 mL**
Olive oil	**2 tbsp.**	**30 mL**
Lime juice	**1 1/2 tbsp.**	**22 mL**
Chopped fresh cilantro or parsley	**1 tbsp.**	**15 mL**
Grated lime zest	**1 1/2 tsp.**	**7 mL**

Preheat gas barbecue to medium. Score both sides of each chicken breast several times with a sharp knife. Combine next 4 ingredients in a small bowl and brush over chicken breasts. Cook chicken on a greased grill for about 6 minutes per side, brushing with lime mixture, until no longer pink inside.

For the salsa, combine remaining 8 ingredients in a small bowl. Serve with chicken. Makes 4 servings.

***1 serving:** 280 Calories; 15 g Total Fat (10 g Mono, 2 g Poly, 2.5 g Sat); 65 mg Cholesterol; 9 g Carbohydrate (1 g Fibre, 7 g Sugar); 27 g Protein; 340 mg Sodium*

Note: If frozen mango is unavailable, use fresh or canned mango instead. Chopped oranges or pineapple also work well.

Tip: Hot peppers contain capsaicin in the seeds and ribs. Removing the seeds and ribs will reduce the heat. Wear rubber gloves when handling hot peppers and avoid touching your eyes. Wash your hands well afterwards.

Beer Can Chicken

Check the barbecue section of your local department store for a roasting stand that is specially made to hold the beer can and chicken safely.

Can of beer (12 1/2 oz., 355 mL)	**1**	**1**
Apple juice	**1/4 cup**	**60 mL**
Apple cider vinegar	**2 tbsp.**	**30 mL**
Cooking oil	**2 tbsp.**	**30 mL**
Worcestershire sauce	**2 tsp.**	**10 mL**
Montreal chicken spice	**2 tbsp.**	**30 mL**
Brown sugar, packed	**2 tsp.**	**10 mL**
Dried oregano	**1 tsp.**	**5 mL**
Dry mustard	**1 tsp.**	**5 mL**
Onion powder	**1 tsp.**	**5 mL**
Whole chicken	**4 lbs.**	**1.8 kg**

Pour 2/3 cup (150 mL) beer into a spray bottle, leaving remaining beer in can. Set can aside. Add next 4 ingredients to spray bottle. Swirl gently to combine. Set aside.

Combine next 5 ingredients in a small bowl. Sprinkle 1 tbsp. (15 mL) seasoning mixture inside chicken cavity. Rub remaining seasoning mixture over surface of chicken. Let stand, covered, in refrigerator for 30 minutes. Stand chicken, tail end down, over beer can and press down to insert can into body cavity. Preheat gas barbecue to medium. Place drip pan under grill on one side of barbecue. Balance chicken upright over drip pan, so that bottom of beer can rests on grill. Turn burner under chicken to low, leaving opposite burner on medium. Close lid. Cook for 1 1/2 to 1 3/4 hours, spraying chicken with beer mixture every 20 minutes, until browned and meat thermometer inserted in thickest part of breast reads 180°F (83°C). Remove chicken from beer can by inserting a carving fork through chicken above level of top of beer can and lifting chicken off of can, taking care not to spill the contents of can, as liquid will be extremely hot. Transfer chicken to a cutting board. Cover with foil and let stand for 10 minutes before carving. Makes 6 servings.

***1 serving:** 570 Calories; 15 g Total Fat (7 g Mono, 3.5 g Poly, 3.5 g Sat); 255 mg Cholesterol; 5 g Carbohydrate (0 g Fibre, 3 g Sugar); 93 g Protein; 930 mg Sodium*

Greek Chicken Thighs

Easy and delicious, the Mediterranean ingredients for this dish offer full-bodied colour and flavour. Hide your best china—guests may want to smash plates in approval as the Greeks used to do.

Large red pepper, halved	**1**	**1**
Large yellow pepper, halved	**1**	**1**
Greek dressing	**2 tbsp.**	**30 mL**
Black olive tapenade	**1/4 cup**	**60 mL**
Plain yogurt	**1/4 cup**	**60 mL**
Boneless, skinless chicken thighs (3 oz., 85 g, each)	**8**	**8**
Large lemon, halved	**1**	**1**
Crumbled feta cheese	**1/2 cup**	**125 mL**
Fresh oregano leaves, lightly packed	**1 tbsp.**	**15 mL**

Grill red and yellow peppers, skin side down, on direct medium-high heat for about 10 minutes until skins are blistered and blackened. Cover with foil and let stand until cool enough to handle. Remove and discard skins. Cut peppers into long strips.

Toss with dressing and set aside.

Combine tapenade and yogurt in a large resealable freezer bag. Add chicken and chill for 30 minutes. Drain and discard marinade. Grill chicken on direct medium heat for about 7 minutes per side until internal temperature reaches 170°F (77°C).

Squeeze lemon over chicken. Sprinkle with cheese and oregano. Serve with grilled peppers. Makes 4 servings.

***1 serving:** 330 Calories; 15 g Total Fat (3 g Mono, 2 g Poly, 5 g Sat); 160 mg Cholesterol; 10 g Carbohydrate (2 g Fibre, 4 g Sugar); 38 g Protein; 540 mg Sodium*

It's worth finding authentic Greek yogurt for this recipe. Greek yogurt is thick and creamy and has no thickening agents added to it, so it is a more natural product than many Northern American yogurts.

Sweet Spice Chicken with Smoky Rhubarb Barbecue Sauce

Tart rhubarb and the smoky heat of chipotle pepper bring gourmet flair to a simple barbecue sauce. Enjoy the sweetness of summer in style!

Chopped rhubarb	**2 cups**	**500 mL**
Dry red wine	**1 cup**	**250 mL**
Brown sugar, packed	**1/2 cup**	**125 mL**
Ketchup	**1/2 cup**	**125 mL**
Cinnamon sticks (4 inches, 10 cm, each)	**2**	**2**
Chopped chipotle pepper in adobo sauce (see Tip, page 96)	**1 tsp.**	**5 mL**
Salt	**1/2 tsp.**	**2 mL**
Brown sugar, packed	**1 tbsp.**	**15 mL**
Ground cinnamon	**1 tsp.**	**5 mL**
Ground ginger	**1 tsp.**	**5 mL**
Ground cloves	**1/2 tsp.**	**2 mL**
Salt	**1/2 tsp.**	**2 mL**
Boneless, skinless, chicken breast halves (about 5 oz., 140 g, each)	**6**	**6**

Combine first 7 ingredients in a saucepan. Gently boil on medium, stirring occasionally, until thickened and reduced by half. Remove and discard cinnamon sticks. Carefully process rhubarb mixture in blender or food processor until smooth (see Safety Tip, below).

Combine next 5 ingredients and rub over chicken. Grill on direct medium heat for about 7 minutes per side until internal temperature reaches 170°F (77°C). Serve with rhubarb mixture. Makes 6 servings.

1 serving: *300 Calories; 2.5 g Total Fat (0 g Mono, 0 g Poly, 0.5 g Sat); 80 mg Cholesterol; 29 g Carbohydrate (1 g Fibre, 26 g Sugar); 33 g Protein; 750 mg Sodium*

Safety Tip: Follow manufacturer's instructions for processing hot liquids.

Coconut Pesto-stuffed Chicken Breasts

Whisk friends to the tropics with chicken breasts stuffed with a coconut pesto. The coconut-rum wash gives the chicken a deep caramelized colour and just a touch of "spirited" flavour.

Fresh basil, lightly packed	**1 1/2 cups**	**375 mL**
Chopped macadamia nuts	**1/3 cup**	**75 mL**
Medium sweetened coconut	**1/3 cup**	**75 mL**
Pineapple juice	**1/4 cup**	**60 mL**
Lime juice	**2 tbsp.**	**30 mL**
Salt	**1/4 tsp.**	**1 mL**
Boneless, skinless chicken breast halves (about 4 oz., 113 g, each)	**4**	**4**
Cooking oil	**1 tsp.**	**5 mL**
Paprika	**1/2 tsp.**	**2 mL**
Seasoned salt	**1/2 tsp.**	**2 mL**
Pepper	**1/4 tsp.**	**1 mL**
Coconut rum	**1/4 cup**	**60 mL**
Brown sugar, packed	**1 1/2 tbsp.**	**22 mL**

In a blender or food processor, process first 6 ingredients until a thick paste forms.

Cut slits horizontally in chicken breasts to form pockets and fill with basil mixture. Secure with wooden picks.

Combine next 4 ingredients and rub over chicken.

Combine rum and brown sugar. Grill chicken on direct medium heat for 5 to 6 minutes per side, brushing occasionally with rum mixture, until chicken is no longer pink inside. Cover with foil and let stand for 5 minutes. Makes 4 servings.

***1 serving:** 310 Calories; 13 g Total Fat (8 g Mono, 1 g Poly, 3.5 g Sat); 65 mg Cholesterol; 12 g Carbohydrate (2 g Fibre, 10 g Sugar); 28 g Protein; 430 mg Sodium*

Lime Chicken and Salsa

These chicken breasts are marinated in a sweet and spicy sauce.

Sweet (or regular) chili sauce	2 tbsp.	30 mL
Peanut (or cooking) oil	1 tbsp.	15 mL
Lime juice	2 tbsp.	30 mL
Finely grated lime zest (see Tip, page 52)	1/2 tsp.	2 mL
Fish sauce	1 tsp.	5 mL
Brown sugar, packed	1 tsp.	5 mL
Finely grated ginger root (or 1/4 tsp., 1 mL, ground ginger)	1 tsp.	5 mL
Garlic clove, minced (or 1/4 tsp., 1 mL, powder)	1	1
Salt	1/4 tsp.	1 mL
Boneless, skinless chicken breast halves (about 1 lb., 454 g)	4	4
Small red pepper, quartered	1	1
Can of pineapple slices (14 oz., 398 mL), drained and 1 tbsp. (15 mL) juice reserved	1	1
Small zucchini, with peel, cut lengthwise into 1/4 inch (6 mm) thick slices	1	1
Lime juice	1 tbsp.	15 mL
Reserved pineapple juice	1 tbsp.	15 mL
Peanut (or cooking) oil	1 tbsp.	15 mL
Chopped salted peanuts	3 tbsp.	45 mL
Garlic clove, minced (or 1/4 tsp., 1 mL, powder)	1	1
Salt	1/4 tsp.	1 mL

For the marinade, combine first 9 ingredients in a resealable freezer bag. Add chicken, seal bag and turn to coat. Let stand in refrigerator for 2 hours to marinate. Drain and discard marinade. Preheat electric grill for 5 minutes or gas barbecue to medium. Cook chicken on a greased grill for about 5 minutes per side until no longer pink inside.

For the salsa, place red pepper, pineapple and zucchini on greased grill. Cook for 5 to 7 minutes, turning once, until grill marks appear and pepper and zucchini are tender-crisp. Finely chop pepper, pineapple and zucchini. Put into a medium bowl.

Stir in remaining 6 ingredients. Makes 4 servings.

1 serving: *250 Calories; 7 g Total Fat (2.5 g Mono, 2 g Poly, 1.5 g Sat); 65 mg Cholesterol; 20 g Carbohydrate (2 g Fibre, 16 g Sugar); 28 g Protein; 330 mg Sodium*

Butterflied Chicken

Excellent roasted flavour in this grilled stuffed chicken.

Butter, softened	**3 tbsp.**	**45 mL**
Worcestershire sauce	**1 tbsp.**	**15 mL**
Liquid honey	**1 tbsp.**	**15 mL**
Lemon pepper	**2 tsp.**	**10 mL**
Dried whole oregano	**3/4 tsp.**	**4 mL**
Garlic cloves, minced (or 1/2 tsp., 2 mL, powder)	**2**	**2**
Whole roasting chicken	**3 1/2 lbs.**	**1.6 kg**

Combine first 6 ingredients in a small bowl.

Place chicken, breast side down, on a cutting board. Using kitchen shears or a sharp knife, cut down both sides of backbone to remove. Turn chicken, breast side up, and press out flat. Carefully loosen, but do not remove, skin from chicken. Stuff butter mixture between flesh and skin, spreading mixture as evenly as possible. Preheat gas barbecue to medium. Turn off centre or left burner. Place chicken, stuffed side down, on a greased grill over a drip pan on unlit side. Close lid and cook for 35 minutes. Carefully turn chicken. Cook for 55 to 60 minutes until meat thermometer inserted in thigh reads 180°F (82°C). Let stand for 15 minutes. Cut into serving-size pieces. Makes 5 servings.

***1 serving:** 600 Calories; 18 g Total Fat (6 g Mono, 2.5 g Poly, 8 g Sat); 290 mg Cholesterol; 5 g Carbohydrate (0 g Fibre, 4 g Sugar); 99 g Protein; 450 mg Sodium*

Spatchcock Chicken: Butterflying is a popular way to cook a whole chicken that allows the bird to cook in a fraction of the time it would take to cook it in its original shape. To butterfly a whole chicken, you cut out the backbone with kitchen shears and lay the bird out flat. This also allows more of the bird to touch the pan, which results in crispier skin. This technique is called butterflying because the meat resembles the shape of a butterfly once it is flattened. Another term for a butterflied whole chicken is a spatchcock chicken. The origin of this colourful term is unclear, but it may date back to 18-century Ireland and be an abbreviation of "dispatch the cock," a phrase tha was used to describe a quick chicken meal. In Australia, spatchcock is also the term used for a young chicken, what we might know as a spring chicken or poussin.

Yakitori

Plan ahead to grill these for family and friends in the late afternoon of a hot summer's day. So quick, you won't miss a moment's conversation.

Mirin	**1/4 cup**	**60 mL**
Thick teriyaki basting sauce	**1/4 cup**	**60 mL**
Chili paste (sambal oelek)	**1 1/2 tsp.**	**7 mL**
Garlic powder	**1/8 tsp.**	**0.5 mL**
Boneless, skinless chicken thighs	**1 lb.**	**454 g**
Bamboo skewers (8 inches, 20 cm, each), soaked in water for 10 minutes	**8**	**8**
Sesame seeds, toasted (see Tip, below)	**1 tsp.**	**5 mL**

Combine first 4 ingredients in a small bowl.

Place chicken between 2 sheets of plastic wrap and pound with a mallet or rolling pin until flattened. Cut in half lengthwise. Place in a medium bowl. Add 1/4 cup (60 mL) mirin mixture and turn chicken until coated. Marinate, covered, in refrigerator for 30 minutes.

Thread chicken, accordion-style, onto skewers. Preheat barbecue to high. Place skewers on a greased grill. Cook for about 2 minutes per side, brushing with remaining mirin mixture, until no longer pink inside.

Sprinkle with sesame seeds. Makes 8 skewers.

***1 skewer:** 100 Calories; 2.5 g Total Fat (0.5 g Mono, 0.5 g Poly, 0.5 g Sat); 45 mg Cholesterol; g Carbohydrate (0 g Fibre, 7 g Sugar); 11 g Protein; 220 mg Sodium*

Tip: When toasting nuts, seeds or coconut, cooking times will vary for each different ingredient—so never toast them together. For small amounts, place the ingredient in an ungreased shallow frying pan. Heat on medium for 3 to 5 minutes, stirring often, until golden. For larger amounts, spread the ingredient evenly in an ungreased shallow pan. Bake in a 350°F (175°C) oven for 5 to 10 minutes, stirring or shaking often, until golden.

Jerk Chicken

Here's a spicy grilled chicken that is easy and fast. Make sure you preheat your grill and clean it off before you cook on it. Increase the chopped jalapeño if you would like this dish to be hotter.

Chopped green onion	**1/2 cup**	**125 mL**
Crushed garlic	**1 tbsp.**	**15 mL**
Chopped jalapeño pepper (see Tip, page 58)	**1 tbsp.**	**15 mL**
Lime juice	**2 tbsp.**	**30 mL**
Olive oil	**2 tbsp.**	**30 mL**
Dried thyme	**1 tsp.**	**5 mL**
Allspice	**1/2 tsp.**	**2 mL**
Coarsely ground pepper	**1/2 tsp.**	**2 mL**
Ground cinnamon	**1/2 tsp.**	**2 mL**
Soy sauce	**2 tsp.**	**10 mL**
Brown sugar	**1 tbsp.**	**15 mL**
Whole chicken, cut into 8 pieces	**1**	**1**

Process first 11 ingredients in a blender or food processor. Pour over chicken and marinate in refrigerator for 2 to 3 hours. Preheat grill for medium-high heat and brush grill grate with oil or spray with a non-stick spray. Cook chicken for 12 to 15 minutes, turning frequently, until chicken juices run clear. Makes 4 servings.

1 serving: *740 Calories; 21 g Total Fat (10 g Mono, 4 g Poly, 4.5 g Sat); 335 mg Cholesterol; 6 g Carbohydrate (0 g Fibre, 4 g Sugar); 124 g Protein; 450 mg Sodium*

Tandoori Chicken Thigh Skewers

Tandoori chicken is truly a culinary gift from our Indian friends. It is traditionally cooked whole on a stick in a Tandoori oven, which can reach 5000°F (2760°C)! Replicating that heat is a bit of a challenge with the domestic barbecues most of us cook with in this country, but this recipe works well with boneless chicken thighs. Serve the skewers with naan bread and rice.

Crushed garlic	**2 tbsp.**	**30 mL**
Finely grated ginger root	**3 tbsp.**	**45 mL**
Canola oil	**3 tbsp.**	**45 mL**
Vinegar	**1 tbsp.**	**15 mL**
Red chili powder or paprika	**1 tbsp.**	**15 mL**
Cardamom seeds	**2 tsp.**	**10 mL**
Ground bay leaves	**2 tsp.**	**10 mL**
Ground cinnamon	**2 tsp.**	**10 mL**
Ground cloves	**2 tsp.**	**10 mL**
Ground ginger	**2 tsp.**	**10 mL**
Plain yogurt	**1 cup**	**250 mL**
Boneless chicken thighs	**3 lbs.**	**1.4 kg**
Bamboo skewers (8 inches, 20 cm, each), soaked in water for 10 minutes	**12**	**12**

Combine first 11 ingredients in a large bowl. Add chicken and marinate in refrigerator for 1 to 3 hours.

Preheat barbecue to medium-high. Skewer chicken, leaving a little space between each piece to allow chicken to cook. Grill for 5 to 7 minutes per side. Turn off heat and close lid. Check skewers after 5 minutes to make sure that chicken is fully cooked (see Tip, below). Makes 7 servings.

***1 serving:** 280 Calories; 11 g Total Fat (4 g Mono, 2.5 g Poly, 2.5 g Sat); 165 mg Cholesterol; 3 g Carbohydrate (0 g Fibre, 1 g Sugar); 39 g Protein; 180 mg Sodium*

Tip: If you do not have an instant-read thermometer to check the chicken thighs for doneness, just cut into the thickest piece. The juices should run clear if the meat is done.

Maple-smoked Chicken Breast

Smoked chicken breasts are great hot or cold, and they're equally great in a chicken salad. Because chicken is so lean, the breasts will dry out if you overcook them. Maple goes well in this dish, but feel free to use honey, molasses or your favourite sweetener, if you prefer.

Kosher salt	**1/4 cup**	**60 mL**
Maple syrup	**1/4 cup**	**60 mL**
Cinnamon stick (4 inches, 10 cm)	**1**	**1**
Water	**4 cups**	**1 L**
Boneless chicken breasts (about 5 oz., 140 g each), skin-on optional	**6**	**6**
Hardwood chips	**1 cup**	**250 mL**

For the brine, bring salt, maple syrup, cinnamon stick and water to a boil in a medium pot. Reduce heat and simmer for 10 minutes. Chill to room temperature, then refrigerate until ice cold.

Add chicken breast and refrigerate for 1 hour per lb. (1/2 hour per kg) of meat. Remove chicken from brine, rinse well with cold water and pat dry. Discard brine.

Place wood chips in middle of a square sheet of foil. Bring corners together to make a pouch. Poke several holes in pouch. Preheat one side of barbecue to medium-low. Place pouch on heated side. When smoke starts to appear from pouch, place chicken breast on off side of barbecue. Close lid and smoke, maintaining a temperature of 300°F (150°C) or less, for about 30 minutes until chicken is cooked. Makes 7 servings.

***1 serving:** 260 Calories; 14 g Total Fat (6 g Mono, 3 g Poly, 4 g Sat); 95 mg Cholesterol; 1 g Carbohydrate (0 g Fibre, 1 g Sugar); 30 g Protein; 990 mg Sodium*

Smoked Chicken Thighs

Make a quick seasoning, massage the thighs with it, smoke them for a couple of hours and they are ready to go. Pairs perfectly with a Caesar or garden salad, but they would also be right at home chopped up into a chicken salad sandwich.

Salt	**1 tbsp.**	**15 mL**
Chopped fresh rosemary	**1 tbsp.**	**15 mL**
Brown sugar	**2 tbsp.**	**30 mL**
Freshly ground black pepper	**1/4 tsp.**	**1 mL**
Paprika	**1 tsp.**	**5 mL**
Garlic powder	**1/2 tsp.**	**2 mL**
Onion powder	**1/2 tsp.**	**2 mL**
Olive oil	**1 tbsp.**	**15 mL**
Bone-in chicken thighs, skin on (about 3 lbs., 1.3 kg, total)	**8**	**8**

Mix first 8 ingredients in a large bowl until they form a paste. Next, toss in thighs and coat evenly with spice paste. Preheat your smoking device to 250°F (120°C) using apple wood. Smoke thighs for about 2 hours, until internal temperature reaches 160°F (71°C) and exterior is browned. Serve right away, or let cool to room temperature before wrapping tightly and refrigerating. Makes 4 servings.

1 serving: *420 Calories; 30 g Total Fat (13 g Mono, 7 g Poly, 9 g Sat); 165 mg Cholesterol; 1 g Carbohydrate (0 g Fibre, 1 g Sugar); 34 g Protein; 1060 mg Sodium*

There is a trick to reheating these thighs. After the smoking is finished, line a small sheet pan with parchment paper and arrange the chicken thighs on it, skin side down. Gently press the flesh side with the palm of your hand, slightly flattening the chicken. This makes the skin side of the chicken flat, ensuring even cooking of the skin. After chilling, use a cast iron pan on medium heat to gently crisp up the skin and heat the thigh through.

Chicken Mole

The chocolate adds a new dimension to this savoury sauce, a staple of Mexican cuisine.

Butter	**1 tbsp.**	**15 mL**
Cooking oil	**1 tbsp.**	**15 mL**
Boneless, skinless chicken breast halves	**1 1/2 lbs.**	**680 g**
Cans of tomato sauce (7 1/2 oz., 213 mL, each)	**2**	**2**
Medium onion, chopped	**1**	**1**
Medium green pepper, chopped	**1**	**1**
Ground almonds	**1/4 cup**	**60 mL**
Whole cloves	**2**	**2**
Chili powder	**2 tsp.**	**10 mL**
Salt	**1 tsp.**	**5 mL**
Pepper	**1/4 tsp.**	**1 mL**
Hot pepper sauce	**1/4 tsp.**	**1 mL**
Garlic powder	**1/4 tsp.**	**1 mL**
Unsweetened chocolate baking square (1 oz., 28 g), cut up	**1/2**	**1/2**

Melt margarine in a frying pan on medium. Add chicken and cook for 4 to 5 minutes per side until browned. Cut into bite-sized pieces. Return to frying pan.

Add next 11 ingredients. Heat, stirring, until mixture is simmering and chocolate is melted. Reduce heat and simmer, covered, for 30 minutes. Makes 6 servings.

1 serving: *240 Calories; 10 g Total Fat (4 g Mono, 2 g Poly, 2.5 g Sat); 70 mg Cholesterol; 11 g Carbohydrate (3 g Fibre, 5 g Sugar); 29 g Protein; 860 mg Sodium*

Parmesan Arugula Piccata

Though piccata (pronounced pih-KAH-tuh) is generally a veal dish, it can also be made with chicken. This recipe is classy enough for company but is also a great option for any night of the week.

Large eggs	**2**	**2**
Fine dry bread crumbs	**3/4 cup**	**175 mL**
Grated Parmesan cheese	**2 tbsp.**	**30 mL**
Garlic powder	**1/2 tsp.**	**2 mL**
Salt	**1/2 tsp.**	**2 mL**
Pepper	**3/4 tsp.**	**4 mL**
Chicken breast cutlets	**1 1/2 lbs.**	**680 g**
Olive oil	**2 tbsp.**	**30 mL**
Finely chopped onion	**1/4 cup**	**60 mL**
Finely chopped arugula, lightly packed	**1/3 cup**	**75 mL**
Prepared chicken broth	**1/3 cup**	**75 mL**

Beat eggs with a fork in a large shallow bowl.

Combine next 5 ingredients on a large plate.

Dip chicken into egg mixture. Press both sides of chicken into crumb mixture until coated. Discard any remaining egg and bread crumb mixtures.

Heat olive oil in a large frying pan on medium. Add chicken and cook for about 5 minutes per side until golden and no longer pink inside. Transfer to a large plate. Cover to keep warm.

Add onion to same frying pan. Cook for about 2 minutes, stirring often, until softened and starting to brown.

Add arugula and broth. Cook, stirring and scraping any brown bits from bottom of pan, until boiling. Drizzle over chicken. Makes 6 servings.

***1 serving:** 260 Calories; 9 g Total Fat (4.5 g Mono, 1 g Poly, 2 g Sat); 140 mg Cholesterol; 3 g Carbohydrate (0 g Fibre, 1 g Sugar); 31 g Protein; 510 mg Sodium*

Frittata Piquante

Kick your day off with this hearty combo of spicy chicken sausage, cheese, potatoes and eggs, all topped with salsa.

Cooking oil	**1 tsp.**	**5 mL**
Uncooked chicken sausage, casing removed	**4 oz.**	**113 g**
Chopped onion	**1/4 cup**	**60 mL**
Diced green pepper	**2 tbsp.**	**30 mL**
Diced cooked unpeeled potato	**1 cup**	**250 mL**
Large eggs, fork-beaten	**2**	**2**
Grated Monterey Jack cheese	**1/2 cup**	**125 mL**
Water	**1 1/2 tbsp.**	**22 mL**
Salt	**1/4 tsp.**	**1 mL**
Pepper, sprinkle		
Salsa (optional)	**2 tbsp.**	**30 mL**

Heat cooking oil in a small frying pan on medium. Add next 3 ingredients and scramble-fry for about 8 minutes until onion is softened.

Add potato and cook for about 2 minutes, stirring often, until heated through.

Combine next 5 ingredients in a small bowl and pour over potato mixture. Stir well. Reduce heat to medium-low. Cook, covered, for about 5 minutes until bottom is golden and top is almost set. Remove from heat. Broil on centre rack in oven (see Tip, below) for about 5 minutes until browned and set.

Spoon salsa over top. Makes 2 servings.

Tip: When baking or broiling food in a frying pan with a handle that isn't ovenproof, wrap the handle in foil and keep it to the front of the oven, away from the element.

1 serving: *380 Calories; 23 g Total Fat (7 g Mono, 2 g Poly, 9 g Sat); 305 mg Cholesterol; 22 g Carbohydrate (2 g Fibre, 3 g Sugar); 22 g Protein; 1140 mg Sodium*

Fajitas

Delicious, nutritous and fun for the whole family! If you prefer your fajitas without peppers, use 2 onions instead.

Cooking oil	1 tbsp.	15 mL
Boneless, skinless chicken breast halves (about 5 oz., 140 g, each), sliced in long thin strips	4	4
Red onion, sliced in rings	1	1
Green pepper, seeded and cut in strips	1	1
Red pepper, seeded and cut in strips	1	1
Yellow pepper, seeded and cut in strips	1	1
Thinly sliced mushrooms	1 cup	250 mL
Salt, sprinkle		
Pepper, sprinkle		
Lemon juice	1 tbsp.	15 mL
Flour tortillas (7 inch, 18 cm), heated in covered bowl	8	8
Grated medium or sharp Cheddar cheese	1 cup	250 mL
Sour cream	1 cup	250 mL
Salsa	1 cup	250 mL
Guacamole	1 cup	250 mL

Heat cooking oil in a frying pan on medium-high. Add chicken and stir-fry until cooked. Transfer to a bowl.

Add next 5 ingredients to same frying pan, adding more cooking oil if needed. Sauté vegetables until browned. Spread on a warm platter.

Return chicken to pan on medium heat. Sprinkle with salt and pepper, and drizzle with lemon juice. Transfer to plate with onion mixture.

Lay 1 tortilla on a plate. Spoon some onion mixture down centre, then a few chicken strips on top. Top with cheese, sour cream, salsa and guacamole. Roll to enclose filling. Makes 8 fajitas.

***1 fajita:** 510 Calories; 22 g Total Fat (6 g Mono, 1.5 g Poly, 11 g Sat); 95 mg Cholesterol; 40 g Carbohydrate (4 g Fibre, 5 g Sugar); 38 g Protein; 950 mg Sodium*

Chicken Ratatouille

In need of a vacation? Send your taste buds on a trip with this robust dish that's full of bold Mediterranean flavours. This versatile dish goes great with crusty bread or pasta. Serve with lemon wedges.

All-purpose flour	**1/4 cup**	**60 mL**
Salt	**1/2 tsp.**	**2 mL**
Pepper	**1/4 tsp.**	**1 mL**
Boneless, skinless chicken thighs (about 3 oz., 85 g, each)	**8**	**8**
Cooking oil	**1 tbsp.**	**15 mL**
Diced eggplant (with peel)	**2 cups**	**500 mL**
Chopped onion	**1 cup**	**250 mL**
Can of diced tomatoes (with juice) (14 oz., 398 mL)	**1**	**1**
Chopped green pepper	**1/2 cup**	**125 mL**
Chopped red pepper	**1/2 cup**	**125 mL**
Sliced fresh white mushrooms	**1 cup**	**250 mL**
Granulated sugar	**1 1/2 tsp.**	**7 mL**
Dried basil	**1 tsp.**	**5 mL**
Dried thyme	**1/2 tsp.**	**2 mL**
Garlic powder	**1/2 tsp.**	**2 mL**
Salt	**1/2 tsp.**	**2 mL**

Combine first 3 ingredients in a large resealable freezer bag. Add chicken and toss until coated. Remove chicken and discard any remaining flour mixture.

Heat cooking oil in a large frying pan on medium-high. Add chicken and cook for about 2 minutes per side until browned. Transfer to a plate.

Add eggplant and onion to same frying pan. Cook for about 5 minutes, stirring often and scraping any brown bits from bottom of pan, until browned and starting to soften.

Stir in remaining 9 ingredients and chicken and bring to a boil. Reduce heat to medium-low and simmer, covered, for about 30 minutes until chicken is no longer pink inside and vegetables are tender. Makes 4 servings.

1 serving: *330 Calories; 10 g Total Fat (4 g Mono, 3.5 g Poly, 2 g Sat); 140 mg Cholesterol; 21 g Carbohydrate (3 g Fibre, 9 g Sugar); 37 g Protein; 1040 mg Sodium*

Thai Chili Soup

Although the coconut milk helps calm the heat a bit, this soup is not for the faint of heart. Thai chilies are much hotter than jalapenos and when combined with the red curry paste, they give this soup a deliciously spicy kick. Feel free to reduce the chilies or red curry paste if you prefer a less spicy dish.

Avocado oil	**1 tbsp.**	**15 mL**
Boneless, skinless chicken breast halves cut into 1 inch (2.5 cm) pieces	**1/2 lb.**	**225 mL**
Avocado oil	**1 tbsp.**	**15 mL**
Thinly sliced onion	**1 cup**	**250 mL**
Garlic cloves, minced	**3**	**3**
Sliced Thai chilies (see Tip, page 58)	**2**	**2**
Minced fresh ginger	**2 tsp.**	**10 mL**
Lemongrass stalks (4 inch, 10 cm, each), Pounded, cut into 2 inch (5 cm) pieces	**2**	**2**
Red Thai curry paste	**2 tsp.**	**10 mL**
Prepared chicken broth	**5 cups**	**1.25 L**
Coconut milk cans (14 oz., 398 mL, each)	**2**	**2**
Sliced mushrooms	**2 cups**	**500 mL**
Lime juice	**3 tbsp.**	**45 mL**
Fish sauce	**1 tbsp.**	**15 mL**
Chopped fresh cilantro	**3 tbsp.**	**45 mL**
Lime slices, for garnish		

Heat avocado oil in a Dutch oven or large pot on medium-high. Add chicken and cook for 3 to 4 minutes, stirring occasionally, until lightly browned. Transfer to a small bowl and set aside.

Heat second amount of avocado oil in same pot on medium. Add onion and cook for 6 to 7 minutes until onion is soft. Stir in next 5 ingredients and cook until fragrant, about 2 minutes.

Add chicken broth and simmer for 30 minutes, stirring occasionally. Remove lemon grass pieces and discard.

Stir in coconut milk, mushrooms and reserved chicken pieces and simmer for 15 to 20 minutes, stirring occasionally, until chicken pieces are cooked through.

Stir in lime juice and fish sauce and cook for another 2 minutes. Sprinkle with cilantro. Garnish individual servings with lime slices. Makes about 12 cups (3 L).

1 cup (250 mL): *180 Calories; 17 g Total Fat (2.5 g Mono, 5 g Poly, 13 g Sat); 10 mg Cholesterol; 5 g Carbohydrate (0 g Fibre, 1 g Sugar); 6 g Protein; 155 mg Sodium*

Meatball Veggie Soup

A soup to use up those bushels of garden zucchini! Tender herbed chicken meatballs taste wonderful with zucchini, peas and mushrooms in a flavourful broth.

Large egg, fork-beaten	**1**	**1**
Fine dry bread crumbs	**1/2 cup**	**125 mL**
Grated Parmesan cheese	**1/3 cup**	**75 mL**
Chopped fresh parsley (or 1 1/2 tsp., 7 mL, flakes)	**2 tbsp.**	**30 mL**
Dried oregano	**1 1/2 tsp.**	**7 mL**
Garlic clove, minced (or 1/4 tsp., 1 mL, dried)	**1**	**1**
Salt	**1/2 tsp.**	**2 mL**
Pepper	**1/4 tsp.**	**1 mL**
Ground chicken	**3/4 lb.**	**340 g**
Cooking oil	**1 tbsp.**	**15 mL**
Sliced fresh white mushrooms	**2 cups**	**500 mL**
Chopped zucchini (with peel)	**1 1/2 cups**	**375 mL**
Chopped onion	**1 cup**	**250 mL**
Salt	**1/2 tsp.**	**2 mL**
Pepper	**1/4 tsp.**	**1 mL**
Prepared chicken broth	**7 cups**	**1.75 L**
Frozen peas	**1 cup**	**250 mL**

Combine first 8 ingredients in a medium bowl.

Add chicken and mix well. Roll into 3/4 inch (2 cm) balls.

Heat cooking oil in a large saucepan on medium-high. Add mushrooms and cook for about 5 minutes, stirring occasionally, until mushrooms are browned and liquid is evaporated.

Stir in next 4 ingredients. Cook for about 5 minutes, stirring often, until onion starts to soften.

Add broth and bring to a boil. Stir in meatballs and bring back to a boil. Reduce heat to medium-low and simmer, covered, for about 15 minutes until meatballs are no longer pink inside.

Stir in peas and cook, covered, for about 4 minutes until peas are heated through. Makes about 10 cups (2.5 L).

1 cup (250mL): *140 Calories; 8 g Total Fat (1.5 g Mono, 0.5 g Poly, 1 g Sat); 50 mg Cholesterol; 7 g Carbohydrate (0 g Fibre, 2 g Sugar); 9 g Protein; 360 mg Sodium*

Chicken Chili

With smoky chipotle peppers, this dish will hold its own at any chili cook-off. Garnish with a dollop of sour cream and a little grated Cheddar cheese and chopped parsley.

Cooking oil	**1 tsp.**	**5 mL**
Ground chicken	**1 lb.**	**454 g**
Chopped celery, optional	**1 cup**	**250 mL**
Chopped red or green pepper	**1 cup**	**250 mL**
Chopped onion	**1 cup**	**250 mL**
Chili powder	**1 tsp.**	**5 mL**
Chopped chipotle peppers in abodo sauce (see Tip, below)	**1 tsp.**	**5 mL**
Garlic powder	**1/4 tsp.**	**1 mL**
Ground cumin	**1/4 tsp.**	**1 mL**
Salt	**1/4 tsp.**	**1 mL**
Pepper	**1/4 tsp.**	**1 mL**
Can of tomato sauce (25 oz., 680 mL)	**1**	**1**
Can of diced tomatoes, drained	**1**	**1**
Can of red kidney beans (14 oz., 398 mL), rinsed and drained	**1**	**1**

Heat oil in a large saucepan or Dutch oven on medium-high. Add next 10 ingredients and scramble-fry for about 5 minutes until chicken is no longer pink.

And remaining 3 ingredients and bring to a boil. Reduce heat to medium-low. Simmer, uncovered, for 2 to 3 minutes until heated through. Makes 6 servings.

***1 serving:** 280 Calories; 5 g Total Fat (0.5 g Mono, 0 g Poly, 0 g Sat); 60 mg Cholesterol; 26 g Carbohydrate (9 g Fibre, 10 g Sugar); 19 g Protein; 1120 mg Sodium*

Tip: Chipotle chili peppers in adobo sauce are smoked jalapeño peppers that are canned in a smoky red sauce. Adobo sauce is not as spicy as the chipotle pepper, but it still packs some heat. Be sure to wash your hands after handling. Store any leftover chipotle peppers in an airtight container in the fridge for up to 1 year.

Chicken Marsala

This casually elegant dish combines tender chicken with mushrooms and Marsala wine. It goes great with buttered noodles with herbs.

Butter	**1 tbsp.**	**15 mL**
Boneless, skinless chicken breast halves (about 5 oz., 140 g, each)	**4**	**4**
Salt, to taste		
Pepper, to taste		
Sliced fresh white mushrooms	**2 cups**	**500 mL**
Prepared chicken broth	**3/4 cup**	**175 mL**
Marsala wine	**1/2 cup**	**125 mL**
Water	**1 tbsp.**	**15 mL**
Cornstarch	**2 tsp.**	**10 mL**
Chopped fresh chives	**1 tbsp.**	**15 mL**

Melt butter in a large frying pan on medium-high. Add chicken and sprinkle with salt and pepper. Cook until all sides of chicken are browned. Transfer to a large plate.

Add mushrooms to same frying pan. Cook for about 5 minutes, stirring occasionally, until mushrooms are softened and liquid is evaporated. Stir in broth and wine and bring to a boil.

Stir water into cornstarch in a small cup until smooth. Add to mushroom mixture. Cook, stirring, until boiling and thickened. Add chicken. Reduce heat to medium-low and simmer, covered, for about 5 minutes, turning chicken occasionally, until heated through. Sprinkle with chives. Makes 4 servings.

1 serving: *240 Calories; 4.5 g Total Fat (1 g Mono, 0.5 g Poly, 2.5 g Sat); 90 mg Cholesterol; 7 g Carbohydrate (0 g Fibre, 3 g Sugar); 34 g Protein; 240 mg Sodium*

Chicken Tetrazzini

A healthier take on a family favourite. A lighter cream sauce reduces the total fat, while whole wheat spaghetti and colourful vegetables add fibre.

Water	**12 cups**	**3 L**
Salt	**1 1/2 tsp.**	**7 mL**
Whole wheat spaghetti, broken in half	**8 oz.**	**225 g**
Canola oil	**2 tsp.**	**10 mL**
Sliced fresh brown (or white) mushrooms	**2 cups**	**500 mL**
Chopped onion	**1 cup**	**250 mL**
Diced red pepper	**1 cup**	**250 mL**
Prepared chicken broth	**1 1/2 cups**	**375 mL**
Dry (or alcohol-free) white wine	**1/4 cup**	**60 mL**
Pepper	**1/4 tsp.**	**1 mL**
Diced cooked chicken breast (see Tip, page 14)	**2 cups**	**500 mL**
Frozen peas, thawed	**1 cup**	**250 mL**
Block light cream cheese, softened	**4 oz.**	**125 g**
Light sour cream	**1/2 cup**	**125 mL**
Grated Parmesan cheese	**1/4 cup**	**60 mL**

Combine water and salt in a Dutch oven and bring to a boil. Add pasta and cook, uncovered, for 10 to 12 minutes, stirring occasionally, until tender but firm. Drain. Return to same pot and cover to keep warm.

Heat canola oil in a large frying pan on medium. Add mushrooms and onion. Cook for about 10 minutes, stirring often, until onion is softened. Stir in red pepper and cook for 2 minutes.

Add next 3 ingredients and bring to a boil.

Stir in next 4 ingredients. Cook for about 5 minutes, stirring occasionally, until heated through. Add pasta and toss well.

Sprinkle with Parmesan cheese. Makes about 7 1/2 cups (1.9 L).

1 cup (250 mL): *290 Calories; 8 g Total Fat (2.5 g Mono, 1.5 g Poly, 3 g Sat); 45 mg Cholesterol; 31 g Carbohydrate (2 g Fibre, 4 g Sugar); 22 g Protein; 280 mg Sodium*

Thai Coconut Chicken

By using lower-fat ingredients, you can enjoy this delicious Thai dish without any guilt! Serve with jasmine or your favourite long-grain rice.

Prepared chicken broth	**1 1/4 cups**	**300 mL**
Lime juice	**3 tbsp.**	**45 mL**
Soy sauce	**2 tbsp.**	**30 mL**
Finely grated ginger root	**1 tbsp.**	**15 mL**
Grated lime zest (see Tip, page 52)	**1 tbsp.**	**15 mL**
Garlic cloves, minced (or 1/2 tsp., 2 mL, powder)	**2**	**2**
Pepper	**1/4 tsp.**	**1 mL**
Boneless, skinless chicken breast halves (about 5oz., 140 g, each)	**4**	**4**
Brown sugar, packed	**1/4 cup**	**60 mL**
Reduced-fat peanut butter	**2 tbsp.**	**30 mL**
Sweet chili sauce	**1 tbsp.**	**15 mL**
Can of light coconut milk (14 oz., 398 mL)	**1**	**1**
Cornsarch	**2 tsp.**	**10 mL**
Grated lime zest, for garnish		
Chopped fresh parsley, for garnish		

Combine first 7 ingredients in a medium frying pan and bring to a boil. Reduce heat to medium.

Add chicken. Cook, covered, for 12 to 15 minutes, turning at halftime, until chicken is no longer pink inside. Transfer chicken to a cutting board and cut into 1 inch (2.5 cm) pieces. Cover to keep warm.

Whisk next 3 ingredients into broth mixture until smooth. Bring to a boil.

Stir coconut milk into cornstarch in a small cup. Slowly add to broth mixture, stirring constantly with whisk, until boiling and slightly thickened. Stir in chicken.

Garnish with lime zest and parsley. Makes 4 servings.

1 serving: *320 Calories; 8 g Total Fat (0 g Mono, 0 g Poly, 2.5 g Sat); 80 mg Cholesterol; 24 g Carbohydrate (2 g Fibre, 18 g Sugar); 37 g Protein; 860 mg Sodium*

Asian Citrus Chicken

Tender chicken and snap peas are so good in this orange sauce. Perfect served over rice.

Orange juice	**3/4 cup**	**175 mL**
Cornstarch	**1 tbsp.**	**15 mL**
Hoisin sauce	**2 tbsp.**	**30 mL**
Oyster sauce	**1 tbsp.**	**15 mL**
Rice vinegar	**1 tbsp.**	**15 mL**
Brown sugar, packed	**2 tsp.**	**10 mL**
Finely grated orange zest (see Tip, page 52)	**1 tsp.**	**5 mL**
Olive oil	**2 tsp.**	**10 mL**
Boneless, skinless chicken breast halves, cut into thin strips	**3/4 lb.**	**340 g**
Garlic cloves, minced (or 1/2 tsp., 2 mL, powder)	**2**	**2**
Ground ginger	**1/2 tsp.**	**2 mL**
Chopped onion	**1 cup**	**250 mL**
Chopped celery	**1 cup**	**250 mL**
Chopped carrot	**2/3 cup**	**150 mL**
Low-sodium prepared chicken broth	**1/2 cup**	**125 mL**
Sugar snap peas, trimmed	**2 cups**	**500 mL**
Sesame seeds, toasted (see Tip, page 72),	**2 tsp.**	**10 mL**

Stir orange juice into cornstarch in a small bowl until smooth. Add next 5 ingredients. Stir well and set aside.

Heat oil in a wok or large non-stick frying pan on medium-high.

Add chicken, garlic and ginger. Stir-fry for about 4 minutes until chicken is no longer pink inside.

Add next 3 ingredients and stir-fry for 2 minutes.

Stir in broth and peas. Reduce heat to medium and boil gently, covered, for 3 to 5 minutes until carrot is tender-crisp and peas are bright green. Stir cornstarch mixture. Add to chicken mixture. Cook, stirring, until mixture is boiling and thickened.

Sprinkle with sesame seeds. Makes 4 servings.

***1 serving:** 225 Calories; 3 g Total Fat (0.5 g Mono, 1 g Poly, 0 g Sat); 50 mg Cholesterol; 26 g Carbohydrate (3 g Fibre, 10 g Sugar); 23 g Protein; 460 mg Sodium*

Polynesian Chicken

Green and red peppers, pineapple chunks and green onion give this sweet and tangy dish a burst of colour. Serve over basmati or other long grain rice.

All purpose flour	**1 cup**	**250 mL**
Cornstarch	**3 tbsp.**	**45 mL**
Salt	**3/4 tsp.**	**4 mL**
Large eggs	**3**	**3**
Water	**4 1/2 tbsp.**	**67 mL**
Boneless, skinless chicken breast halves cut into 3/4 inch (2 cm) pieces, about 2 cups (500 mL)	**1 lb.**	**454 g**
Cooking oil, for deep frying		
Reserved pineapple juice	**1/4 cup**	**60 mL**
Cornstarch	**2 tsp.**	**10 mL**
Ketchup	**1/3 cup**	**75 mL**
White vinegar	**3 tbsp.**	**45 mL**
Dry sherry	**2 tbsp.**	**30 mL**
Water	**1 tbsp.**	**15 mL**
Cooking oil	**1 tbsp.**	**15 mL**
Chopped red pepper	**1 cup**	**250 mL**
Chopped green pepper	**1 cup**	**250 mL**
Can of pineapple tidbits (14 oz., 398 mL), drained and 1/4 cup (60 mL) juice reserved	**1**	**1**
Sliced green onions	**3 tbsp.**	**45 mL**

For the batter, stir first 3 ingredients in a medium bowl. Make a well in center.

Beat eggs and water with a fork in a small bowl. Add to well. Stir until mixture has consistency of medium-thick batter with only a few lumps.

Add chicken and stir until coated. Transfer, 1 piece at a time with tongs, to hot (375°F, 190°C) oil in a deep fryer or large pot. Deep fry, in 3 or 4 batches, for about 5 minutes per batch, turning occasionally, until golden brown on all sides and chicken is no longer pink inside. Transfer to paper towels to drain.

For the sauce, stir pineapple juice into cornstarch in a small bowl. Add next 4 ingredients and stir well. Set aside.

Heat wok or a large frying pan on medium-high until very hot. Add cooking oil. Add peppers and stir-fry for about 3 minutes until peppers are tender-crisp. Stir in pineapple. Stir sauce and add to wok. Cook, stirring, until thickened. Add chicken and stir until coated. Sprinkle with green onions. Makes about 4 cups (1 L).

1/2 cup (125 mL): *250 Calories; 8 g Total Fat (4.5 g Mono, 2 g Poly, 1 g Sat); 35 mg Cholesterol; 28 g Carbohydrate (1 g Fibre, 12 g Sugar); 15 g Protein; 390 mg Sodium*

Chicken in Coconut Curry Sauce

Also known as Kuku Paku, this is a popular dish in East Africa, such as Tanzania and Kenya. In Swahili Kuku means Chicken and Paku means smear. If you want a more authentic flavour, feel free to barbecue the chicken before putting it into the curry sauce.

Chopped Roma tomatoes	**3**	**3**
Chopped serrano chilies, seeded	**2**	**2**
Chopped white onion	**1**	**1**
Piece of ginger root (3 inches, 7.5 cm), peeled	**1**	**1**
Garlic cloves, peeled	**4**	**4**
Cilantro leaves	**1/4 cup**	**60 mL**
Smoked paprika	**1/2 tsp.**	**2 mL**
Salt	**1/2 tsp.**	**2 mL**
Chili powder	**1/4 tsp.**	**1 mL**
Whole chicken, cut into 8 pieces skin removed	**4 lbs.**	**1.8 kg**
Olive oil	**2 tbsp.**	**30 mL**
Ground coriander	**3/4 tsp.**	**4 mL**
Turmeric	**1/2 tsp.**	**2 mL**
Salt	**1/2 tsp.**	**2 mL**
Ground cumin	**1/4 tsp.**	**1 mL**
Can of coconut milk (14 oz., 398 mL)	**1**	**1**
Lemon juice	**3 tbsp.**	**45 mL**
Cilantro leaves, for garnish		
Lemon wedges, for garnish		

Combine first 9 ingredients in a blender or food processor. Blend until smooth.

Place chicken and 1 cup (250 mL) tomato mixture into a resealable bag. Set rest of tomato mixture aside. Seal bag and turn to coat chicken with mixture. Let stand in refrigerator for 1 to 2 hours to marinate. Transfer chicken to a prepared baking sheet skin side up and discard marinade. Bake in 350°F (175°C) oven for 35 to 40 minutes. Broil chicken for another 5 to 10 minutes until browned and internal temperature reaches 170°F (77°C).

While chicken is cooking, heat oil in a Dutch oven to medium. Add spices and cook, stirring constantly, until fragrant, about 1 to 2 minutes. Add reserved tomato mixture to Dutch oven and stir. Cook, stirring occasionally, until moisture is evaporated, about 20 minutes.

Whisk in coconut milk and bring to a simmer. Simmer, stirring frequently, for 15 to 20 minutes until sauce has slightly thickened. Whisk in lemon juice. Add chicken and juices from pan. Cook for another 5 minutes to allow flavours to combine and chicken to warm through.

Serve with cilantro and lemon wedges. Makes 6 servings.

1 serving: *430 Calories; 9 g Total Fat (0 g Mono, 0 g Poly, 3 g Sat); 90 mg Cholesterol; 26 g Carbohydrate (4 g Fibre, 19 g Sugar); 42 g Protein; 890 mg Sodium*

Chicken and Pea Risotto

This creamy risotto has a delicious smoky bacon and roast chicken flavour—perfect for dinner.

Prepared chicken broth	**4 cups**	**1 L**
Olive (or cooking) oil	**1 tbsp.**	**15 mL**
Butter (or hard margarine)	**1 tbsp.**	**15 mL**
Finely chopped onion	**1 cup**	**250 mL**
Garlic cloves, minced (or 1/2 tsp., 2 mL, powder)	**2**	**2**
Arborio rice	**1 cup**	**250 mL**
Dry white (or alcohol-free) wine	**1/2 cup**	**125 mL**
Chopped leftover cooked chicken (about 6 oz., 170 g)	**1 cup**	**250 mL**
Frozen peas	**1 cup**	**250 mL**
Sour cream	**1/4 cup**	**60 mL**
Bacon slices, cooked crisp and crumbled	**4**	**4**
Arugula, lightly packed	**1 cup**	**250 mL**
Finely grated fresh Parmesan cheese	**1/4 cup**	**60 mL**
Chopped fresh parsley (or 2 1/4 tsp., 11 mL, flakes)	**3 tbsp.**	**45 mL**

Pour broth into a medium saucepan and bring to a boil. Reduce heat to low and cover.

Heat olive oil and butter in a large saucepan on medium. Add onion and garlic and cook for 5 to 10 minutes, stirring often, until onion is softened.

Add rice to garlic mixture and stir until rice is well coated. Add wine. Cook, stirring, for about 1 minute until wine is absorbed. Add 3/4 cup (175 mL) broth, stirring constantly, until absorbed. Repeat with remaining broth, 3/4 cup (175 mL) at a time, until all liquid is absorbed. This will take about 25 minutes.

Add next 4 ingredients. Cook, stirring, for about 5 minutes until heated through. Remove from heat. Stir in arugula.

Stir in Parmesan cheese and parsley. Makes about 4 1/2 cups (1.1 L).

1 cup (250 mL): *250 Calories; 6 g Total Fat (2.5 g Mono, 1 g Poly, 2 g Sat); 105 mg Cholesterol; 24 g Carbohydrate (4 g Fibre, 4 g Sugar); 21 g Protein; 610 mg Sodium*

Chicken Teriyaki

No need for expensive take-out when you can make this delicious dish at home. Serve over hot jasmine or your favourite long grain rice.

Soy sauce	**1/4 cup**	**60 mL**
Sake (rice wine) or sherry or fruit juice	**1/4 cup**	**60 mL**
Brown sugar, packed	**3 tbsp.**	**45 mL**
Ground ginger	**1/2 tsp.**	**2 mL**
Garlic powder	**1/4 tsp.**	**1 mL**
Dry mustard	**1/8 tsp.**	**0.5 mL**
Pepper	**1/4 tsp.**	**1 mL**
Boneless, skinless chicken breast halves (about 1 lb., 454 g), cut into strips	**4**	**4**
Cooking oil	**1 tbsp.**	**15 mL**
Slivered onion	**1 cup**	**250 mL**
Sesame seeds, toasted (see Tip, page 72), for garnish	**1 1/2 tsp.**	**7 mL**
Thinly sliced green onion, for garnish	**1**	**1**

Combine first 7 ingredients in a medium bowl.

Add chicken and turn until well coated. Marinate in refrigerator for about 20 minutes.

Heat wok or frying pan until hot. Add cooking oil. Add onion and stir-fry for 2 minutes. Add chicken and marinade. Reduce heat and simmer, covered, for 10 to 12 minutes until chicken is no longer pink.

Sprinkle with sesame seeds and green onion. Makes 4 servings.

1 serving: *240 Calories; 5 g Total Fat (2.5 g Mono, 1.5 g Poly, 0.5 g Sat); 65 mg Cholesterol; 15 g Carbohydrate (0 g Fibre, 11 g Sugar); 29 g Protein; 1000 mg Sodium*

Chicken Biryani

Curried chicken and vividly coloured rice flavoured with saffron and cilantro, topped with sweet tomatoes and almonds. Top with a cinnamon stick or two for a lovely presentation.

Ghee	**1 tbsp.**	**15 mL**
Boneless, skinless chicken thighs, cut into bite-sized pieces	**1 lb.**	**454 g**
Salt, sprinkle		
Pepper, sprinkle		
Ghee	**1 tbsp.**	**15 mL**
Chopped onion	**1 cup**	**250 mL**
Garlic cloves, minced	**2**	**2**
Finely grated ginger root	**1 tsp.**	**5 mL**
Basmati rice	**1 1/2 cups**	**375 mL**
Mild curry paste	**1 tbsp.**	**15 mL**
Cinnamon stick (4 inches, 10 cm)	**1**	**1**
Dried crushed chilies	**1/2 tsp.**	**2 mL**
Saffron threads	**1/2 tsp.**	**2 mL**
Whole green cardamom, bruised	**3**	**3**
Prepared chicken broth	**2 1/2 cups**	**625 mL**
Ghee	**2 tsp.**	**10 mL**
Sliced natural almonds	**1/4 cup**	**60 mL**
Can of petite diced tomatoes (19 oz., 540 mL), drained	**1**	**1**

Heat first amount of ghee in a Dutch oven on medium-high. Add chicken and sprinkle with salt and pepper. Cook until no longer pink inside, about 5 minutes, and transfer to a plate.

Add second amount of ghee to pot and reduce heat to medium. Add next 3 ingredients and cook until onion starts to soften, about 5 minutes. Add rice and stir until coated.

Add next 5 ingredients and cook, stirring, until fragrant. Add broth and chicken and bring to a boil. Cook, covered, for 15 minutes, without lifting lid, until rice is tender. Remove from heat and let stand for 5 minutes until any liquid is absorbed.

Heat remaining ghee in a frying pan on medium. Add almonds and stir-fry for 3 minutes until starting to brown. Add tomatoes and stir for 1 minute. Spoon rice mixture into a serving dish and top with tomato mixture. Makes about 6 cups (1.5 L).

1 cup (250 mL): *370 Calories; 14 g Total Fat (2 g Mono, 1 g Poly, 4.5 g Sat); 75 mg Cholesterol; 42 g Carbohydrate (3 g Fibre, 6 g Sugar); 22 g Protein; 700 mg Sodium*

Saffron stigmas, or threads, grow from a small purple crocus found in many parts of Europe and Asia. It takes over 14,000 stigmas to produce 1 oz (28 g) of saffron. Fortunately, a small amount of saffron will flavour a large amount of food. Buy whole saffron threads rather than ground to ensure you are getting a top-quality product.

Mexi Mac and Cheese

Looking for some creamy comfort food? Try this version of a pasta classic that adds chicken bacon, black beans, salsa and Mexican cheese blend for some fiesta flair.

Water	**12 cups**	**3 L**
Elbow macaroni	**3 cups**	**750 mL**
Canned black beans, rinsed and drained	**1 cup**	**250 mL**
Salsa	**2 cups**	**500 mL**
Can of kernel corn (19 oz., 549 mL), drained	**1**	**1**
Can of condensed cream of mushroom soup (10 oz., 284 mL)	**1**	**1**
Chopped green pepper	**1 cup**	**250 mL**
Cooked, crumbled chicken bacon	**1/2 lb.**	**225 g**
Grated Mexican cheese blend	**1 cup**	**250 mL**

Bring water to a boil in a Dutch oven. Add pasta and cook, uncovered, for 8 to 10 minutes, stirring occasionally, until tender but firm. Drain and return to pot. Cover to keep warm.

Meanwhile, combine next 5 ingredients in a large saucepan. Bring to a boil on medium-high, stirring often. Stir in bacon and cook, stirring occasionally, until bacon is heated through. Add to pasta and stir gently.

Sprinkle with cheese and let stand, covered, for about 5 minutes until cheese is melted. Makes about 10 1/2 cups (2.6 L).

***1 cup (250 mL):** 330 Calories; 11 g Total Fat (1 g Mono, 0.5 g Poly, 2 g Sat); 35 mg Cholesterol; 40 g Carbohydrate (5 g Fibre, 6 g Sugar); 17 g Protein; 770 mg Sodium*

Festive Chicken Bake

Festive Chicken Bake cries out to be eaten with family and friends. It is a true comfort food best enjoyed during the cold winter months when relatives stop by from out of town. We like to serve this dish on Boxing Day or around New Year's because, for a lack of a better description, it's a meal that sticks to your ribs and feels good in your tummy. The hint of cranberry and orange will remind you of warm summer days not so far off.

All-purpose flour	**3 tbsp.**	**45 mL**
Salt	**1/4 tsp.**	**1 mL**
Pepper	**1/8 tsp.**	**0.5 mL**
Paprika	**1/8 tsp.**	**0.5 mL**
Boneless, skinless chicken breast halves (about 5 oz., 140 g, each)	**6**	**6**
Cooking oil	**1 tbsp.**	**15 mL**
Prepared chicken broth	**1/2 cup**	**125 mL**
Fresh or frozen cranberries	**1 cup**	**250 mL**
Frozen concentrated orange juice, thawed	**1/3 cup**	**75 mL**
Diced onion	**1/4 cup**	**60 mL**
Ground cinnamon	**1/4 tsp.**	**1 mL**
Ground ginger	**1/4 tsp.**	**1 mL**

Combine flour, salt, pepper and paprika in a large resealable plastic bag. Add chicken and toss until coated. Remove chicken, reserving remaining flour mixture.

Heat oil in a large frying pan on medium-high. Add chicken and cook for 2 to 3 minutes per side until browned. Arrange chicken in a single layer in a greased 2 quart (2 L) shallow baking dish.

Preheat oven to 350°F (175°C). In a small bowl, combine chicken broth and reserved flour mixture. Stir in remaining 5 ingredients. Pour over chicken. Bake, covered, for about 45 minutes, until fully cooked. Makes 6 servings.

***1 serving:** 230 Calories; 4 g Total Fat (2 g Mono, 1 g Poly, 0.5 g Sat); 80 mg Cholesterol; 12 g Carbohydrate (1 g Fibre, 7 g Sugar); 34 g Protein; 240 mg Sodium*

Sunday Fried Chicken

For those who prefer to wade rather than sink when they're frying, we've "shallow fried" then baked this crispy chicken delight just for you. Start marinating on Saturday for dinner on Sunday—and don't forget a side of coleslaw.

Bone-in chicken thighs (about 5 oz., 140, each)	**6**	**6**
Chicken drumsticks (about 4 oz. 113 g, each)	**6**	**6**
Buttermilk	**1 1/2 cups**	**375 mL**
Water	**1 1/2 cups**	**375 mL**
Louisiana hot sauce	**1 tbsp.**	**15 mL**
Soy sauce	**1 tbsp.**	**15 mL**
Worcestershire sauce	**1 tsp.**	**5 mL**
Garlic powder	**1/2 tsp.**	**2 mL**
All-purpose flour	**1 cup**	**250 mL**
Onion powder	**1 tsp.**	**5 mL**
Salt	**1 tsp.**	**5 mL**
Pepper	**1/2 tsp.**	**2 mL**
Baking powder	**1/2 tsp.**	**2 mL**
Cayenne pepper	**1/2 tsp.**	**2 mL**
Poultry seasoning	**1/2 tsp.**	**2 mL**
Seasoned salt	**1 tsp.**	**5 mL**
Cooking oil, approximately	**3 cups**	**750 mL**

Put chicken into a large resealable freezer bag.

Combine next 6 ingredients in a small bowl. Pour over chicken. Seal bag and turn until chicken is well coated. Let stand in refrigerator for 12 to 24 hours, turning occasionally. Remove chicken. Do not pat dry. Discard any remaining buttermilk mixture.

Combine next 7 ingredients in a separate large resealable freezer bag. Add chicken in batches, tossing until coated. Discard any remaining flour mixture. Place chicken on a baking sheet and let stand for 10 minutes.

Sprinkle chicken with seasoned salt. Heat 1/2 inch (12 mm) cooking oil in a large frying pan or large pot on medium-high until hot. Add half of chicken pieces. Cook for about 3 minutes per side until golden. Transfer to a wire rack set in a baking sheet with sides. Repeat with remaining chicken.

Bake chicken in 375°F (190°C) oven for 20 to 30 minutes until fully cooked and internal temperature reaches 170°F (77°C). Makes 6 servings.

1 serving: *540 Calories; 36 g Total Fat (17 g Mono, 8 g Poly, 8 g Sat); 160 mg Cholesterol; 17 g Carbohydrate (1 g Fibre, 0 g Sugar); 36 g Protein; 850 mg Sodium*

Chicken Cordon Bleu

This classic dish combines a creamy centre of ham and Swiss cheese wrapped in a tender chicken breast that has been breaded and pan-fried until golden and crispy. Perfection!

Boneless, skinless chicken breast halves (about 5 oz., 140 g, each)	**6**	**6**
Salt	**1/2 tsp.**	**2 mL**
Deli cooked ham slices (about 6 oz., 170 g, total)	**6**	**6**
Swiss cheese, cut into 6 sticks	**6 oz.**	**170 g**
All purpose flour	**1/2 cup**	**125 mL**
Eggs, fork beaten	**2**	**2**
Dijon mustard	**2 tbsp.**	**30 mL**
Panko bread crumbs	**1 cup**	**250 m**
Garlic powder	**1 tsp.**	**5 mL**
Salt	**1/2 tsp.**	**2 mL**
Pepper	**1/2 tsp.**	**2 mL**
Cooking oil	**3 tbsp.**	**45 mL**

Pound chicken with a mallet to 1/4 inch (6 mm) thickness. Sprinkle with salt.

Lay 1 ham slice on top of 1 chicken piece. Lay 1 cheese stick over ham and roll up, jelly-roll style, tucking in sides. Secure with wooden picks. Repeat with remaining chicken, ham, and cheese.

Place flour in a shallow bowl. Whisk egg and Dijon mustard together in another shallow dish. Combine panko bread crumbs, garlic powder, salt and pepper in another shallow dish. Press 1 roll into flour, shaking off excess. Dip roll into egg mixture and then press into panko mixture, covering roll completely. Set aside. Repeat with remaining rolls

Heat 2 tbsp. (30 mL) oil in a large frying pan on medium. Add half of chicken rolls and cook until golden on each side, about 3 minutes per side. Transfer to a prepared 2 quart (2 L) baking dish. Repeat with remaining rolls, adding remaining oil, if neccessay. Bake in a 350°F (175°C) oven for about 25 to 30 minutes, until just cooked through. Carefully remove wooden picks and serve. Makes 6 servings.

***1 serving:** 450 Calories; 19 g Total Fat (5 g Mono, 2.5 g Poly, 7 g Sat); 200 mg Cholesterol; 18 g Carbohydrate (0 g Fibre, 0 g Sugar); 50 g Protein; 890 mg Sodium*

Bacon Wrapped Chicken with Asparagus

Boneless, skinless chicken breast halves (about 5 oz., 140 g, each)	**6**	**6**
Grated Havarti cheese	**3/4 cup**	**175 mL**
Asparagus spears, about 5 inches (12.5 cm) long	**18**	**18**
Slices of roasted red pepper, about 6 inches (15 cm) long	**12**	**12**
Garlic powder	**1 tsp.**	**5 mL**
Paprika	**3/4 tsp.**	**4 mL**
Salt	**1/2 tsp.**	**2 mL**
Bacon slices	**6**	**6**

Place 1 chicken breast between 2 sheets of plastic wrap. Pound with a mallet or rolling pin to 1/2 inch (12 mm) thickness. Place 2 tbsp. (30 mL) cheese, 3 asparagus spears and 2 slices of pepper onto chicken, leaving about 1/2 inch (12 mm) border. Roll up tightly, jelly-roll style. Repeat with remaining chicken breasts.

Combine next 3 ingredients in a small bowl and sprinkle over chicken. Wrap a slice of bacon tightly around chicken breast. Secure with a wooden pick and place on a prepared baking sheet. Bake in 375°F (190°C) oven for about 30 minutes until fully cooked and internal temperature reaches 170°F (77°C). Remove wooden picks and serve. Makes 6 servings.

***1 serving:** 400 Calories; 23 g Total Fat (9 g Mono, 2.5 g Poly, 9 g Sat); 120 mg Cholesterol; 4 g Carbohydrate (1 g Fibre, 2 g Sugar); 42 g Protein; 740 mg Sodium*

Bourbon Glazed Chicken

Serve this tender, seasoned chicken with its sweet glaze on a bed of long grain white rice. Add a fresh garden salad for a complete meal.

Bourbon	**1 cup**	**250 mL**
Ketchup	**2/3 cup**	**150 mL**
Brown sugar	**1/2 cup**	**125 mL**
White wine vinegar	**1/4 cup**	**60 mL**
Garlic cloves, minced	**3**	**3**
Worcestershire sauce	**2 tbsp.**	**30 mL**
Lemon juice	**1 tbsp.**	**15 mL**
Dry mustard	**1/2 tsp.**	**2 mL**
Salt	**1/2 tsp.**	**2 mL**
Pepper	**1/2 tsp.**	**2 mL**
All-purpose flour	**3 tbsp.**	**45 mL**
Crushed dried rosemary	**1 tsp.**	**5 mL**
Salt	**1/4 tsp.**	**1 mL**
Pepper	**1/8 tsp.**	**0.5 mL**
Paprika	**1/8 tsp.**	**0.5 mL**
Boneless, skinless, chicken breast halves (about 5 oz., 140 g, each)	**6**	**6**
Cooking oil	**1 tbsp.**	**15 mL**

Combine first 10 ingredients in a medium saucepan. Bring to a boil, and then reduce heat and simmer for 8 to 10 minutes, stirring occasionally, until glaze is slightly thickened. Set aside.

Combine next 5 ingredients in a large resealable freezer bag. Add chicken and toss until coated. Remove chicken, discarding remaining flour.

Heat cooking oil in a large frying pan on medium. Add chicken. Cook for 2 to 3 minutes per side until brown. Arrange in a single layer in a greased 2 quart (2 L) shallow casserole dish. Pour bourbon glaze over chicken. Bake, covered, in 350°F (175°C) oven for about 40 minutes until fully cooked and internal temperature reaches 170°F (77°C). Makes 6 servings.

***1 serving:** 380 Calories; 4 g Total Fat (2 g Mono, 1 g Poly, 0.5 g Sat); 80 mg Cholesterol; 30 g Carbohydrate (0 g Fibre, 26 g Sugar); 33 g Protein; 900 mg Sodium*

Classic Chicken Pot Pie

This pot pie is the ultimate in comfort food—the perfect meal for a blustery day. Serve with a side of roasted broccoli or sauteed spinach.

Boneless, skinless chicken thighs	**1 lb.**	**454 g**
Prepared chicken broth	**2 1/2 cups**	**625 mL**
Butter (or hard margarine)	**2 tbsp.**	**30 mL**
Sliced fresh white mushrooms	**2 cups**	**500 mL**
Sliced leek (white part only)	**2 cups**	**500 mL**
Thinly sliced carrot	**1 1/2 cups**	**375 mL**
Thinly sliced celery	**3/4 cup**	**175 mL**
All-purpose flour	**1/4 cup**	**60 mL**
Dried rosemary, crushed	**1/4 tsp.**	**1 mL**
Dried thyme	**1/4 tsp.**	**1 mL**
Salt	**1/2 tsp.**	**2 mL**
Pepper	**1/4 tsp.**	**1 mL**
Dry sherry	**3 tbsp.**	**45 mL**
Package of puff pastry (14 oz., 397 g), thawed according to package directions	**1/2**	**1/2**
Large egg, fork-beaten	**1**	**1**

In a medium saucepan, bring chicken and broth to a boil. Reduce heat to low and simmer, covered, for about 15 minutes until chicken is no longer pink inside. Transfer chicken with a slotted spoon to a cutting board, reserving broth. Cut into 3/4 inch (2 cm) pieces.

Melt butter in a large frying pan on medium. Add next 4 ingredients. Cook for about 10 minutes, stirring occasionally, until vegetables are tender-crisp.

Add next 5 ingredients and cook, stirring, for 1 minute. Slowly add sherry and reserved broth, stirring constantly until smooth. Cook, stirring, for about 5 minutes until boiling and thickened. Stir in chicken. Transfer to a greased 2 quart (2 L) baking dish. Let stand for about 30 minutes until cool.

Roll out puff pastry on a lightly floured surface to fit baking dish. Place over baking dish and press pastry against sides to seal. Gently brush egg over pastry. Cut several small vents in top to allow steam to escape. Bake in 400°F (200°C) oven for about 25 minutes until filling is bubbling and pastry is puffed and golden. Makes 4 servings.

1 serving: *590 Calories; 31 g Total Fat (14 g Mono, 4 g Poly, 10 g Sat); 160 mg Cholesterol; 43 g Carbohydrate (4 g Fibre, 6 g Sugar); 31 g Protein; 980 mg Sodium*

Coconut-crusted Chicken

These chicken breasts are stuffed with spinach and feta and can be served with or without an accompanying sauce of your choice. For added convenience, you can prepare this recipe in advance, leaving only the baking for your last-minute meal preparations.

Cooking oil	**1/2 tsp.**	**2 mL**
Finely chopped onion	**1/2 cup**	**125 mL**
Curry powder	**1 tsp.**	**5 mL**
Chopped fresh spinach leaves, lightly packed	**2 cups**	**500 mL**
Crumbled feta cheese	**1/2 cup**	**125 mL**
Boneless, skinless chicken breast halves (about 5 oz, 140 g, each)	**6**	**6**
Fine coconut	**3/4 cup**	**175 mL**
Finely chopped salted cashews	**3/4 cup**	**175 mL**
Chopped fresh parsley	**1 tbsp.**	**15 mL**
Large eggs	**2**	**2**
All-purpose flour	**1/2 cup**	**125 mL**
Curry powder	**1 tbsp.**	**15 mL**
Salt	**1/2 tsp.**	**2 mL**

Heat cooking oil in a medium frying pan on medium. Add onion and curry powder. Cook for about 5 minutes, stirring often, until onion is softened.

Add spinach and cook for about 2 minutes, stirring occasionally, until spinach is wilted and no liquid remains. Transfer to a small bowl. Add cheese and stir until cheese is melted. Chill for about 1 hour until cold.

Cut a horizontal slit in thickest part of each chicken breast to create a pocket. Fill with spinach mixture.

Combine next 3 ingredients in a large shallow dish. Beat eggs with a fork in a medium shallow bowl. Combine remaining 3 ingredients on a large plate. Coat chicken in flour mixture, shaking off any excess. Dip into egg • and press into coconut mixture until coated. Discard any remaining flour mixture, egg and coconut mixture. Arrange on a greased foil-lined baking sheet with sides (see Note). Cook in 375°F (190°C) oven for about 25 minutes until internal temperature of chicken reaches 170°F (77°C). Temperature of stuffing should reach at least 165°F (74°C). Let stand for 5 minutes. Makes 6 servings.

1 serving: *390 Calories; 17 g Total Fat (2 g Mono, 1 g Poly, 5 g Sat); 165 mg Cholesterol; 16 g Carbohydrate (2 g Fibre, 3 g Sugar); 42 g Protein; 460 mg Sodium*

Note: You can prepare the chicken to this point up to 4 hours in advance. Chill, covered, until ready to cook.

Spinach Chicken Lasagna

With lots of sauce, rich flavours and a tempting appearance, this dish is sure to best its beef brother.

Cooking oil	**1 1/2 tbsp.**	**22 mL**
Boneless, skinless chicken breast halves, chopped	**1 3/4 lbs.**	**790 g**
Sliced fresh white mushrooms	**2 cups**	**500 mL**
Chopped onion	**1 1/2 cups**	**375 mL**
Chopped red pepper	**1 1/2 cups**	**375 mL**
Garlic cloves, minced (or 1/2 tsp., 2 mL, powder)	**2**	**2**
Tomato pasta sauce	**4 cups**	**1 L**
Chopped fresh spinach leaves, lightly packed	**2 cups**	**500 mL**
Can of diced tomatoes (14 oz., 398 mL), with juice	**1**	**1**
Dried oregano	**2 tsp.**	**10 mL**
Dried basil	**1 tsp.**	**5 mL**
Salt	**1/4 tsp.**	**1 mL**
Pepper	**1/8 tsp.**	**0.5 mL**
Cayenne pepper (optional)	**1/4 tsp.**	**1 mL**
2% cottage cheese	**1 1/2 cups**	**375 mL**
Crumbled feta cheese	**1/2 cup**	**125 mL**
Grated Parmesan cheese	**1/3 cup**	**75 mL**
Dried thyme	**1/2 tsp.**	**2 mL**
Pepper	**1/2 tsp.**	**2 mL**
Dried rosemary, crushed	**1/4 tsp.**	**1 mL**
Cooked spinach lasagna noodles	**12**	**12**
Grated mozzarella and Cheddar cheese blend	**2 cups**	**500 mL**
Parsley flakes	**2 tsp.**	**10 mL**

Heat cooking oil in a Dutch oven or large pot on medium-high. Add chicken and cook for 8 to 10 minutes, stirring occasionally, until no longer pink. Transfer to a plate. Reduce heat to medium.

Add next 4 ingredients to same pot. Cook for about 10 minutes, stirring often, until onion is softened.

Stir in next 8 ingredients and chicken. Simmer, covered, for 10 minutes, stirring occasionally, to blend flavours. Remove from heat. Set aside.

Combine next 6 ingredients in a medium bowl. To assemble, layer ingredients in a greased 9 x 13 inch (23 x 33 cm) baking pan as follows: 1 cup (250 mL) chicken mixture, 3 lasagna noodles, 3 cups (750 mL) chicken mixture, 3 lasagna noodles, cottage cheese mixture, 3 lasagna noodles, 3 cups (750 mL) chicken mixture, 3 lasagna noodles and remaining chicken mixture.

Combine cheese blend and parsley in a medium bowl. Sprinkle over top. Cover with greased foil and bake in 350°F (175°F) oven for 60 minutes. Remove foil. Bake for another 30 minutes until cheese is bubbling and starting to turn golden. Let stand for 10 minutes before serving. Makes 8 servings.

1 serving: *520 Calories; 17 g Total Fat (5 g Mono, 1.5 g Poly, 8 g Sat); 100 mg Cholesterol; 46 g Carbohydrate (6 g Fibre, 11 g Sugar); 45 g Protein; 1380 mg Sodium*

Classic Roast Chicken

Every cook needs a recipe for a perfectly cooked roast chicken complete with stuffing and a savoury homemade gravy.

Whole roasting chicken	**6 lbs.**	**2.7 kg**
Coarse dry bread crumbs	**6 cups**	**1.5 L**
Dry onion flakes	**1/4 cup**	**60 mL**
Parsley flakes	**1 tbsp.**	**15 mL**
Poultry seasoning	**2 tsp.**	**10 mL**
Celery salt	**1/2 tsp.**	**2 mL**
Salt	**1 tsp.**	**5 mL**
Pepper	**1/4 tsp.**	**1 mL**
Butter (or hard margarine), melted	**1/4 cup**	**60 mL**
Water, approximately	**1 1/2 cups**	**375 mL**
Chicken fat (or cooking oil), skimmed from drippings	**1/2 cup**	**125 mL**
All-purpose flour	**1/2 cup**	**125 mL**
Salt	**1 tsp.**	**5 mL**
Pepper	**1/4 tsp.**	**1 mL**
Drippings, plus water to make	**4 cups**	**1 L**

Tie wings close to chicken body with butcher's string.

For the stuffing, combine next 7 ingredients in a large bowl.

Add butter and water. Stir well. Add a bit more water, if needed, until stuffing is moist and holds together when squeezed. Loosely fill body cavity of chicken with stuffing. Secure with wooden picks or small metal skewers. Tie legs to tail. Transfer to a medium roaster. Cook, covered, in 400°F (200°C) oven for 20 minutes. Reduce heat to 325°F (160°C). Cook for 2 to 2 1/2 hours until tender and meat thermometer reads 180°F (82°C). Remove cover for last few minutes of cooking to brown chicken, if needed. Remove stuffing. Let stand, tented with foil, for 10 minutes before carving. If you prefer to cook uncovered, be sure to baste often.

For the gravy, stir chicken fat into flour, salt and pepper in a medium saucepan until smooth. Add drippings and water. Cook, stirring, on medium until boiling and thickened. Serve with chicken. Makes 8 servings.

1 serving: *1100 Calories; 35 g Total Fat (14 g Mono, 6 g Poly, 9 g Sat); 305 mg Cholesterol; 77 g Carbohydrate (4 g Fibre, 4 g Sugar); 119 g Protein; 1880 mg Sodium*

Springtime Chicken Pizza

This cheesy chicken pizza, topped with lots of veggies, is destined to become a year-round favourite.

Prebaked pizza crust (12 inch, 30 cm, diameter)	**1**	**1**
Pizza sauce	**1/3 cup**	**75 mL**
Grated Parmesan cheese	**1/2 cup**	**125 mL**
Chopped cooked chicken	**1 1/2 cups**	**375 mL**
Roasted red peppers, drained, blotted dry, cut into strips	**1/3 cup**	**75 mL**
Fresh asparagus spears, trimmed of tough ends	**8**	**8**
Goat (chèvre) cheese, cut up	**2/3 cup**	**150 mL**

Preheat oven to 475°F (240°C). Place pizza crust on a greased 12 inch (30 cm) pizza pan. Spread pizza sauce evenly on crust. Sprinkle with Parmesan cheese.

Scatter chicken and red pepper over Parmesan cheese.

Arrange asparagus spears in a spoke pattern on top of red pepper. Scatter goat cheese over top. Bake for about 15 minutes until crust is crisp and golden. Cuts into 8 wedges.

***1 wedge:** 200 Calories; 8 g Total Fat (2 g Mono, 0.5 g Poly, 4 g Sat); 35 mg Cholesterol; 17 g Carbohydrate (1 g Fibre, 2 g Sugar); 16 g Protein; 390 mg Sodium*

Chicken Parmesan

Spoon this chicken over a bed of spaghetti or fettucini with a Caesar salad on the side, or serve it alongside some creamy mashed potatoes and roasted broccoli.

All-purpose flour	**1/2 cup**	**125 mL**
Eggs, fork beaten	**2**	**2**
Grated Parmesan cheese	**1/2 cup**	**125 mL**
Fine dry bread crumbs	**3/4 cup**	**175 mL**
Dried oregano	**1/2 tsp.**	**2 mL**
Garlic powder	**1/4 tsp.**	**1 mL**
Salt	**1 tsp.**	**5 mL**
Pepper	**1/4 tsp.**	**1 mL**
Boneless, skinless chicken breast halves (about 5 oz., 140 g, each)	**6**	**6**
Olive oil	**3 tbsp.**	**45 mL**
Prepared tomato sauce	**1 2/3 cups**	**400 mL**
Grated mozzarella cheese	**1 2/3 cups**	**400 mL**
Grated Parmesan cheese	**2/3 cup**	**150 mL**

Put flour into a shallow bowl. Whisk eggs in a separate shallow bowl. Combine next 6 ingredients in a third shallow bowl.

Dip chicken breasts into flour, shaking off excess. Next, dip chicken into eggs, allowing excess egg to drip off. Roll in crumb mixture until coated. Set aside on a large plate.

Heat 2 tbsp. (30 mL) oil in a medium frying pan on medium heat. Cook 3 chicken breasts until brown on both sides, about 3 minutes per side. Repeat with remaining oil and chicken. Transfer to a greased 9 x 13 (23 x 33 cm) baking dish.

Top each chicken breast with about 1/3 cup (75 mL) tomato sauce, 1/3 cup (75 mL) mozzarella and 2 tbsp. (30 mL) Parmesan. Bake in 400°F (200°C) oven for 25 to 30 minutes until cheese is bubbling and melted and chicken is cooked through. Makes 6 servings.

1 serving: *490 Calories; 19 g Total Fat (6 g Mono, 1.5 g Poly, 8 g Sat); 185 mg Cholesterol; 25 g Carbohydrate (2 g Fibre, 4 g Sugar); 51 g Protein; 1460 mg Sodium*

Chicken Provençal

Tender chicken with a complex tomato sauce and plenty of peppers and olives. This saucy main course can be served with potatoes or over your favourite pasta or rice.

All-purpose flour	**1/3 cup**	**75 mL**
Salt	**1/4 tsp.**	**1 mL**
Pepper	**1/2 tsp.**	**2 mL**
Bone-in chicken thighs (about 5 oz., 140 g, each), skin removed	**8**	**8**
Olive (or cooking) oil	**1 tbsp.**	**15 mL**
Sliced fresh white mushrooms	**1 1/2 cups**	**375 mL**
Chopped green pepper	**1/2 cup**	**125 mL**
Chopped onion	**1/2 cup**	**125 mL**
Garlic cloves, minced (or 1/2 tsp., 2 mL, powder)	**2**	**2**
Dry (or alcohol-free) white wine	**1/2 cup**	**125 mL**
Can of diced tomatoes (with juice) (14 oz., 398 mL)	**1**	**1**
Dried marjoram	**1 tsp.**	**5 mL**
Granulated sugar	**1/4 tsp.**	**1 mL**
Chopped kalamata olives (optional)	**2 tbsp.**	**30 mL**

Combine first 3 ingredients in large resealable freezer bag. Add chicken. Seal bag. Toss until coated. Transfer chicken to plate. Reserve remaining flour mixture.

Heat olive oil in a large frying pan on medium-high. Add chicken. Cook for about 5 minutes, turning occasionally, until browned. Transfer with a slotted spoon to an ungreased 3 quart (3 L) casserole. Reduce heat to medium.

Add next 4 ingredients to same frying pan. Cook for about 5 minutes, stirring often, until liquid is evaporated. Sprinkle with reserved flour mixture. Cook, stirring, for 1 minute.

Add wine and cook, stirring and scraping any brown bits from bottom of pan, until boiling. Stir in next 3 ingredients. Pour over chicken. Cook, covered, in 350°F (175°C) oven for about 35 minutes until internal temperature of chicken reaches 170°F (77°C).

Sprinkle with olives. Makes 4 servings.

1 serving: *410 Calories; 13 g Total Fat (6 g Mono, 2.5 g Poly, 3 g Sat); 190 mg Cholesterol; 17 g Carbohydrate (2 g Fibre, 5 g Sugar); 48 g Protein; 690 mg Sodium*

Parmesan Wings

Perfect for when you just want something deliciously messy for dinner! Serve this with fries, and don't forget the napkins!

Plain yogurt	**3/4 cup**	**175 mL**
Chicken drumettes (or whole chicken wings, split in half and tips discarded)	**3 lbs.**	**1.4 kg**
Grated Parmesan cheese	**1 1/2 cups**	**375 mL**
Fine dry bread crumbs	**1/3 cup**	**75 mL**
Parsley flakes	**1 1/2 tsp.**	**7 mL**
Paprika	**1 1/2 tsp.**	**7 mL**
Seasoned salt	**1 1/2 tsp.**	**7 mL**

Measure yogurt into an extra-large bowl. Add chicken and stir until coated.

Combine remaining 5 ingredients in a large resealable freezer bag. Add 1/3 of chicken. Seal bag and toss until coated. Repeat twice with remaining 2/3 of chicken. Put chicken into a greased 3 1/2 to 4 quart (3.5 to 4 L) slow cooker. Cook, covered, on Low for 8 to 9 hours or on High for 4 to 4 1/2 hours. Transfer chicken with a slotted spoon to a large serving platter. Discard liquid. Makes 4 servings.

***1 serving:** 950 Calories; 67 g Total Fat (3 g Mono, 0.5 g Poly, 23 g Sat); 290 mg Cholesterol; 12 g Carbohydrate (0 g Fibre, 4 g Sugar); 77 g Protein; 1480 mg Sodium*

Tipsy Chicken and Olives

A great dish to eat during winter. Serve over cooked brown rice to soak up the tasty gravy.

Canola oil	**2 tsp.**	**10 mL**
Boneless, skinless chicken breasts, (about 4 oz.,113 g, each), cut in half	**4**	**4**
Sliced onion	**1 cup**	**250 mL**
Sliced shallots	**1/2 cup**	**125 mL**
Chopped celery	**1 cup**	**250 mL**
Chopped carrot	**1 cup**	**250 mL**
Garlic cloves, minced	**2**	**2**
Pale ale	**1 cup**	**250 mL**
Prepared low-sodium chicken broth	**1 1/2 cups**	**375 mL**
Frozen peas	**1 cup**	**250 mL**
Fresh rosemary sprigs	**2**	**2**
Garlic and herb no-salt seasoning	**1 tsp.**	**5 mL**
Pepper	**1/2 tsp.**	**2 mL**
Green olives pitted	**1 cup**	**250 mL**
Chopped fresh rosemary	**2 tbsp.**	**30 mL**

Heat oil in a large frying pan on medium-high. Add chicken and cook for about 8 minutes, stirring occasionally, until browned on all sides. Transfer with a slotted spoon to a 4 to 5 quart (4 to 5 L) slow cooker.

Add next 5 ingredients to same frying pan. Cook for about 5 minutes, stirring often, until onion starts to soften.

Add beer, scraping any browned bits from bottom of pot. Transfer to slow cooker.

Stir in next 5 ingredients. Cook, covered, on Low for 7 to 8 hours, or on High for 3 1/2 to 4 hours.

Discard rosemary sprigs and add green olives and fresh rosemary. Makes 4 servings.

***1 serving:** 340 Calories; 7 g Total Fat (3.5 g Mono, 1 g Poly, 0.5 g Sat); 85 mg Cholesterol; 25 g Carbohydrate (3 g Fibre, 8 g Sugar); 40 g Protein; 820 mg Sodium*

The Best Chicken Dish

An outstanding slow cooker meal that's perfect served with rice or pasta. It can be prepared the night before by browning the ground chicken, chopping the veggies and refrigerating everything in separate containers for easy assembly in the morning.

Cooking oil	**1 tbsp.**	**15 mL**
Ground chicken	**1 lb.**	**454 g**
Can of chickpeas (garbanzo beans), (19 oz., 540 mL), rinsed and drained	**1**	**1**
Finely chopped onion	**1 cup**	**250 mL**
Salt	**1/4 tsp.**	**1 mL**
Sun-dried tomato pesto	**1/3 cup**	**75 mL**
All-purpose flour	**1 tbsp.**	**15 mL**
Can of diced tomatoes (with juice) (14 oz., 398 mL)	**1**	**1**
Balsamic vinegar	**1 tbsp.**	**15 mL**
Granulated sugar	**1/2 tsp.**	**2 mL**
Salt	**1/4 tsp.**	**1 mL**
Chopped red pepper	**4 cups**	**1 L**
Finely chopped zucchini (with peel)	**1 cup**	**250 mL**

Heat cooking oil in a large frying pan on medium. Add ground chicken and scramble-fry for 5 to 10 minutes until no longer pink. Drain well. Transfer to a 3 1/2 to 4 quart (3.5 to 4 L) slow cooker.

Stir in next 3 ingredients.

Stir pesto into flour in a medium bowl until smooth. Add next 4 ingredients. Stir well. Pour over chicken mixture. Stir well. Cook, covered, on Low for 8 to 10 hours or on High for 4 to 5 hours.

Stir in red pepper and zucchini. Cook, covered, on High for 30 to 45 minutes until red pepper is tender-crisp. Makes 8 servings.

***1 serving:** 260 Calories; 13 g Total Fat (1 g Mono, 0.5 g Poly, 0.5 g Sat); 45 mg Cholesterol; 21 g Carbohydrate (5 g Fibre, 8 g Sugar); 15 g Protein; 550 mg Sodium*

Mushroom Chicken Sauce

This delicious sauce cooks while you're out and about. Put some pasta on when you get home and dinner's on the table in minutes!

Bacon slices, diced	**6**	**6**
Cooking oil	**1 tbsp.**	**15 mL**
Chopped onion	**1 cup**	**250 mL**
Sliced fresh white mushrooms	**3 cups**	**750 mL**
Paprika	**1 tsp.**	**5 mL**
Garlic cloves, minced (or 1/2 tsp., 2 mL, powder)	**2**	**2**
All-purpose flour	**3 tbsp.**	**45 mL**
Salt	**1/4 tsp.**	**1 mL**
Pepper	**1/4 tsp.**	**1 mL**
Boneless, skinless chicken thighs, cut into 3/4 inch (2 cm) cubes	**1 1/2 lbs.**	**680 g**
Dry (or alcohol-free) white wine	**1/2 cup**	**125 mL**
Prepared chicken broth	**1/2 cup**	**125 mL**
Frozen peas	**1/2 cup**	**125 mL**
Chopped fresh parsley (or 1 tbsp., 15 mL, flakes)	**1/4 cup**	**60 mL**
Sour cream	**1/4 cup**	**60 mL**

Cook bacon in a large frying pan on medium for about 5 minutes, stirring occasionally, until almost crisp. Transfer with a slotted spoon to paper towels to drain. Drain and discard drippings from pan.

Heat cooking oil in same frying pan on medium. Add onion and cook for 5 to 10 minutes, stirring often, until softened.

Add next 3 ingredients. Cook for about 5 minutes, stirring occasionally, until mushrooms are softened. Stir in bacon. Spread mixture evenly in a 3 1/2 to 4 quart (3.5 to 4 L) slow cooker.

Combine next 3 ingredients in a large resealable freezer bag. Add chicken, seal bag and toss until chicken is coated. Arrange chicken over mushroom mixture. Discard any remaining flour mixture.

Pour wine and broth over chicken. Cook, covered, on Low for 8 to 9 hours or on High for 4 to 4 1/2 hours.

Stir in remaining 3 ingredients. Cook, covered, on High for about 10 minutes until heated through. Makes about 5 1/4 cups (1.3 L).

1 cup (250 mL): *470 Calories; 30 g Total Fat (13 g Mono, 4.5 g Poly, 9 g Sat); 140 mg Cholesterol; 11 g Carbohydrate (2 g Fibre, 3 g Sugar); 34 g Protein; 660 mg Sodium*

Chicken Fricassee

Any fine French chef will tell you that fricassee is meat stewed in a white cream sauce. But never worry that this dish will pale by comparison—the carrot, red pepper and peas add nice shots of colour.

Chopped carrot	**2 cups**	**500 mL**
Chopped celery	**1 1/2 cups**	**375 mL**
Chopped red or orange pepper	**1 1/2 cups**	**375 mL**
Boneless, skinless chicken breast halves, halved	**1 lb.**	**454 g**
Boneless, skinless chicken thighs	**1 lb.**	**454 g**
Sliced leek (white part only)	**3 1/2 cups**	**875 mL**
Butter (or hard margarine)	**3 tbsp.**	**45 mL**
Garlic cloves, minced (or 1/2 tsp., 2 mL, powder), optional	**2**	**2**
All-purpose flour	**1/4 cup**	**60 mL**
Prepared chicken broth	**2 cups**	**500 mL**
Dry (or alcohol-free) white wine	**1/4 cup**	**60 mL**
Can of artichoke hearts (14 oz., 398 mL), drained and halved	**1**	**1**
Dried thyme	**1 tsp.**	**5 mL**
Seasoned salt	**1 tsp.**	**5 mL**
Pepper	**1/4 tsp.**	**1 mL**
Frozen peas	**2 cups**	**500 mL**
Can of evaporated milk (5 1/2 oz., 160 mL)	**1**	**1**

Layer first 6 ingredients, in order given, in a 4 to 5 quart (4 to 5 L) slow cooker.

Melt butter in a medium saucepan on medium. Add garlic and cook, stirring, for about 1 minute until fragrant.

Add flour and cook, stirring, for 1 minute.

Slowly add broth and wine, stirring constantly, until smooth. Cook, stirring, for about 7 minutes until boiling and thickened. Remove from heat.

Stir in next 4 ingredients and pour over chicken mixture in slow cooker. Cook, covered, on Low for 8 to 9 hours or on High for 4 to 4 1/2 hours.

Stir in peas and evaporated milk. Cook, covered, on High for about 15 minutes until peas are tender. Makes 8 servings.

***1 serving:** 300 Calories; 9 g Total Fat (2.5 g Mono, 1 g Poly, 4.5 g Sat); 100 mg Cholesterol; 22 g Carbohydrate (5 g Fibre, 9 g Sugar); 31 g Protein; 750 mg Sodium*

Apple Cabbage Chicken

Tender chicken in a rich, savoury sauce with lovely apple notes—the perfect pairing for the traditional-tasting combination of bacon and cabbage. Serve this dish with steamed baby potatoes.

Shredded green cabbage, lightly packed	**3 cups**	**750 mL**
Bacon slices, chopped	**4**	**4**
Boneless, skinless chicken thighs, trimmed of fat, halved	**2 lbs.**	**900 g**
Salt	**1/4 tsp.**	**1 mL**
Pepper	**1/4 tsp.**	**1 mL**
Sliced onion	**1 cup**	**250 mL**
Garlic cloves, minced (or 1/2 tsp., 2 mL, powder)	**2**	**2**
Apple cider	**1 cup**	**250 mL**
Apple cider vinegar	**2 tbsp.**	**30 mL**
Dijon mustard (with whole seeds)	**1 tbsp.**	**15 mL**
Dried dillweed	**2 tsp.**	**10 mL**
Dried thyme	**1/2 tsp.**	**2 mL**
Salt	**1/4 tsp.**	**1 mL**
Pepper	**1/4 tsp.**	**1 mL**
Frozen peas, thawed	**1 cup**	**250 mL**
Grated peeled tart apple (such as Granny Smith)	**1 cup**	**250 mL**

Put cabbage into a 3 1/2 to 4 quart (3.5 to 4 L) slow cooker.

Cook bacon in a large frying pan on medium until crisp. Transfer with a slotted spoon to a plate lined with paper towel to drain. Discard all but 1 tsp. (5 mL) drippings.

Sprinkle chicken with salt and pepper. Add to same frying pan and cook, in 2 batches, for about 2 minutes per side, until browned. Transfer with a slotted spoon to slow cooker. Reduce heat to medium.

Add onion and garlic to same frying pan. Cook for about 5 minutes, stirring often, until onion is softened.

Combine next 7 ingredients in a small bowl. Add to onion mixture. Cook, stirring and scraping any brown bits from bottom of pan, until boiling. Pour over chicken. Scatter bacon over top. Cook, covered, on Low for 5 to 6 hours or on High for 2 1/2 to 3 hours.

Add peas and apple. Stir gently. Cook, covered, on High for about 15 minutes until heated through. Makes about 6 cups (1.5 L).

1 cup (250 mL): *370 Calories; 18 g Total Fat (7 g Mono, 3 g Poly, 5 g Sat); 145 mg Cholesterol; 16 g Carbohydrate (3 g Fibre, 11 g Sugar); 35 g Protein; 610 mg Sodium*

Raspberry Chicken

Rah, rah raspberry! Three cheers for this MVI (most valuable ingredient). Sweet yet tangy, all the stats agree—this dish is a sure winner!

Raspberry jam	**1/2 cup**	**125 mL**
Dry (or alcohol-free) white wine	**1/3 cup**	**75 mL**
Raspberry red wine vinegar	**1/4 cup**	**60 mL**
Soy sauce	**1 tbsp.**	**15 mL**
Dijon mustard	**1 tsp.**	**5 mL**
Bay leaves	**2**	**2**
Garlic clove, minced (or 1/4 tsp., 1 mL, powder)	**1**	**1**
Chicken legs, back attached (about 11 oz., 310 g, each), skin removed	**4**	**4**
Water	**2 tbsp.**	**30 mL**
Cornstarch	**1 tbsp.**	**15 mL**
Chopped fresh parsley, for garnish		

Combine first 7 ingredients in a small bowl. Transfer to a large resealable freezer bag. Add chicken. Seal bag. Turn until coated. Let stand in refrigerator for at least 4 hours or overnight, turning occasionally. Transfer chicken with raspberry mixture to a 1 1/2 to 2 quart (1.5 to 2 L) slow cooker. Cook, covered, on Low for 6 to 8 hours or High for 3 to 4 hours. Transfer chicken to a serving dish with a slotted spoon or tongs. Cover to keep warm. Skim fat from sauce.

Stir water into cornstarch in a small cup. Add to slow cooker and stir well. Cook, covered, on High for about 5 minutes until boiling and thickened. Pour over chicken.

Garnish with parsley. Makes 4 servings.

1 serving: *520 Calories; 16 g Total Fat (4.5 g Mono, 4 g Poly, 4 g Sat); 250 mg Cholesterol; 29 g Carbohydrate (0 g Fibre, 24 g Sugar); 60 g Protein; 530 mg Sodium*

Country Chicken Stew

This "thyme-ly" meal can be made ahead so it is ready to eat when you are! The night before, prepare the vegetables (except the potato) and the broth mixture. Chill overnight in separate covered bowls. In the morning, assemble and cook as directed. Serve this delicately seasoned, hearty stew in bread bowls.

Chopped onion	**1 cup**	**250 mL**
Chopped potato (with skin)	**2 cups**	**500 mL**
Sliced carrot	**2 cups**	**500 mL**
Shredded green cabbage, lightly packed	**2 cups**	**500 mL**
Chopped celery	**1/2 cup**	**125 mL**
Boneless, skinless chicken thighs	**3 1/2 lbs.**	**1.6 kg**
Prepared chicken broth	**2 cups**	**500 mL**
Can of condensed cream of mushroom soup (10 oz., 284 mL)	**1**	**1**
Dried thyme	**1 tsp.**	**5 mL**
Salt	**1 1/2 tsp.**	**7 mL**
Pepper	**1 1/2 tsp.**	**7 mL**
Bay leaves	**2**	**2**
Prepared chicken broth	**1/4 cup**	**60 mL**
Cornstarch	**1/4 cup**	**60 mL**
Frozen peas	**1 cup**	**250 mL**

Layer first 6 ingredients, in order given, in a 5 to 7 quart (5 to 7 L) slow cooker.

Combine next 5 ingredients in a medium bowl and pour over chicken. Add bay leaves. Do not stir. Cook, covered, on Low for 9 to 10 hours or on High for 4 1/2 to 5 hours. Remove and discard bay leaves.

Stir second amount of broth into cornstarch in a small cup until smooth. Add to chicken mixture. Add peas and stir well. Cook, covered, on High for 15 to 20 minutes until peas are heated through and sauce is thickened. Makes 14 servings.

***1 serving:** 210 Calories; 6 g Total Fat (1.5 g Mono, 1.5 g Poly, 1.5 g Sat); 95 mg Cholesterol; 13 g Carbohydrate (2 g Fibre, 3 g Sugar); 24 g Protein; 620 mg Sodium*

Index